■SCHOLASTIC

D1309572

Collaborative
ART & WRITING PROJECTS
for Young Learners

15 Delightful Projects That Build Early Reading and Writing Skills—and Connect to the Topics You Teach

by **CHRISTY HALE**

New York • Toronto • London • Auckland • Sydney
Mexico City • New Delhi • Hong Kong • Buenos Aires

Teaching *Resources*

For Brooklyn Friends School teachers
Sharon Carter, Shari Lee Cancel, Linda Herman, and Michael Bruno
with gratitude for the opportunities for collaboration
in your classrooms—C.H.

"A teacher affects eternity; he can never tell where his influence stops."
HENRY BROOKS ADAMS, "On Teaching," 1907

Scholastic Inc. grants teachers permission to photocopy the pattern
pages from this book for classroom use. No other part of this publication
may be reproduced in whole or in part, or stored in a retrieval system,
or transmitted in any form or by any means, electronic, mechanical,
photocopying, recording, or otherwise, without written permission
of the publisher. For information regarding permission, write to
Scholastic Inc., 557 Broadway, New York, NY 10012-3999

Cover design by Maria Lilja
Interior design and illustration by Christy Hale
Photographs by Doug Peck

ISBN—13: 978-0-439-43462-1
ISBN—10: 0-439-43462-9

Copyright © 2006 by Christy Hale
All rights reserved. Published by Scholastic Inc.
Printed in the U.S.A.

1 2 3 4 5 6 7 8 9 10   40   14 13 12 11 10 09 08 07 06

Contents

About This Book

When young children begin school, the idea of sharing, waiting their turn, and listening to others is often a new experience. This is why learning how to collaborate is such an important social skill for children in the early grades. When we provide children who have diverse backgrounds and developmental levels with opportunities to participate in collaborative group activities, we foster in them self-respect and an appreciation and tolerance for different points of view.

The 15 art and writing projects in this book provide opportunities for the productive collaboration of the children in your class. From impressive wall displays to 3-D constructions to foldout books, the activities help children explore and work with many media. In addition, the "visual language" of the art projects serves as a wonderful springboard for the writing component, providing a forum for children to exchange information and ideas. As they create collaborative poems, informational science books, sensory descriptions, rhyming advertising jingles, and more, children will build vocabulary, sharpen writing skills, and explore the richness and possibilities of language. And because the projects connect with many favorite early childhood themes, including neighborhood and community, transportation, the farm, insects, and the water cycle, children will build important background knowledge as well.

Enjoy these projects with the children in your class, and know that you will be helping them not only develop important literacy skills but also use their imagination and creativity and build classroom community.

The lesson for each project in this book takes you from preparation to finished product. Here's an overview of what you'll find:

Getting Started: Suggestions for discussion and activities to introduce the theme of the project to children.

Book Links: A list of age-appropriate books and Web sites you can use to help children learn more about the topic before they begin each project.

Materials: A complete list of all supplies and tools that are needed for each project, as well as possible substitutions.

Steps: Step-by-step instructions with clear, supportive illustrations to guide you through the process. (In addition, color photographs that show how the completed projects might look appear in the middle of this book.)

Tips: Helpful management suggestions for breaking down each project into parts that can be completed by children working in small groups over several days or sessions.

Templates: Reproducible patterns for children to use accompany some of the projects.

Writing Connection: Easy-to-do writing activities culminate each of the projects. Children collaborate to write poems, informational books, and ads and jingles, and explore vivid language, point of view, and more.

Helpful Tips

Following are some tips to help develop rich art and writing experiences in your classroom.

Art Projects

- If possible, try out the projects before doing them with children. This will help you to identify needed materials and tools; familiarize yourself with the steps; designate work, drying, and storage areas; and assess the amount of time you'll need, including time for preparation, setup, and cleanup. Gather and prepare materials for each project ahead of time. Assign helpers to distribute and collect materials.

- The projects in this book can be made with materials that are easy to find in the classroom or at home. Consider preparing a send-home letter asking families and caregivers to help you gather materials for projects by saving items at home and bringing them to the classroom. Items might include:

  - cornhusks (saved and dried after shucking)
  - clean, empty milk cartons, egg cartons, cereal and cracker boxes, and shoe boxes
  - used manila folders and cardboard
  - plastic bags
  - magazines and newspapers
  - paper towel and bathroom tissue rolls
  - fabric scraps (prints and solids)
  - string and yarn
  - paper bags
  - cotton balls
  - bubble wrap
  - styrofoam packing peanuts and other types of packing materials
  - aluminum foil
  - old toothbrushes (Make sure these are sterilized before use.)

- Paper plates, paper bowls, or styrofoam food trays make handy containers for paint. To hold water for rinsing paintbrushes, clear, plastic food containers work well. (Remind children always to rinse paintbrushes before using a new color of paint.)

- To avoid wasting paint when children blend colors, encourage them first to mix together a dab of each color. When they achieve the desired result, they can make a larger amount.

- Some of the projects include half patterns. Photocopy the templates onto heavyweight paper or cardboard to make them easier for children to handle. To use the half patterns, show children how to place the template against the folded edge of a piece of folded paper and then cut out the shape, beginning the cut at the fold.

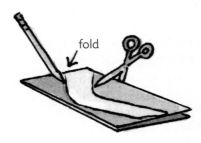

- Cover work areas with newspaper to minimize cleanup. Old shower curtains or plastic tablecloths also work well and can be easily wiped down after use.

- To keep children's clothing clean, use aprons, smocks, old shirts, or trash bags with holes cut for heads and arms. (Always supervise children's use of plastic bags.)

- Provide wet paper towels or premoistened wipes for easy cleaning of messy hands.

The Writing Connection

The art projects in this book are natural motivators for inspiring children to write. A project such as Water Cycle Go-Round (page 48), for example, offers a multitude of visual details for children to use as a basis for expanding their vocabulary and incorporating descriptive language in their writing.

Before children begin writing, model for them what they are expected to do. In the Writing Connection activity for Water Cycle Go-Round, for example, children practice using onomatopoeia—words that sound like their meanings. A sample mini-lesson follows:

1. Begin by encouraging children to reflect on what they learned about the phases of the water cycle and the ways in which they showed this information in their water cycle book. Invite them to share as you record their responses on chart paper.

2. Next, do a think-aloud to demonstrate how a writer might transform some of this information, such as *When a cloud becomes full of water vapor, the vapor turns into droplets and falls as rain.* "What does rain sound like when it begins to fall? I know that when raindrops first hit the leaves on trees, they make a gentle sound. What words do I know that might describe this? How about *pitter-patter*? Then they come down harder: *plop!*" Then you might write something like *Pitter-patter, plop! Rain pours down from the clouds.* Explain that words such as *pitter-patter* and *plop* sound like their meaning.

3. Demonstrate a few more examples and then invite volunteers to think aloud using information on the chart paper. Encourage them to come up with other words to describe the sounds of rain, water, and snow in different phases of the water cycle, such as *splat, gurgle, slosh,* and *slurp*. Then let children try their hand at using onomatopoeia in their writing.

- To help children with their writing, develop word walls (at children's eye level) with lists of words related to each topic to help build word recognition, assist in word analysis, aid in spelling, and expand vocabulary.

- You can build on children's writing experience by encouraging them to practice reading what they've written until they can read it fluently. Choral reading works well for collaborative poems and story retellings. Another useful strategy is echo reading, in which children repeat text read by you, incorporating proper tone, expression, and pacing.

Meeting the Language Arts Standards

The activities in this book are designed to support you in meeting the following recommendations and goals for early reading and writing put forth in a joint position statement by the International Reading Association (IRA) and the National Association for the Education of Young Children (NAEYC). These goals describe a continuum for children's development in grades K–2:
- engages in and talks about reading and writing experiences
- uses descriptive language to explain and explore
- retells simple stories or informational books
- has opportunities for independent reading and writing practice
- reads, writes, and discusses a range of different text types, such as poems and informational books
- writes about topics that are personally meaningful
- builds lists of commonly used words from their writing and reading.

Source: *Learning to Read and Write: Developmentally Appropriate Practices for Young Children*
© 1998 by The National Association for the Education of Young Children.

Incredible Insects

Invite children to learn about insects and then show off their new knowledge by creating imaginary insects that creep, crawl, leap, and fly in a beautiful garden. Continue the fun with a collaborative list poem that uses alliterative language.

Getting Started

1. To activate prior knowledge and provide background information about insects, begin by sharing some of the resources suggested in Book Links and the Web site, below. (Always supervise children's use of the Internet.) Then ask questions, such as "What is an insect? Where do insects live? How are they different from each other? How are they alike?" (*There are thousands and thousands of different kinds of insects, but they share certain attributes: three body parts and six legs; some insects also have wings and antennae.*)

2. Tell children that they are going to design and create insects that live in a beautiful garden.

Tip: *This project can be done over four days (or four sessions). Begin with the sky and grass. Then make the flowers, soil, and insects. Finally, assemble the parts of the display.*

Book Links

Are You an Ant? **(Backyard Books)** by Judy Allen (Kingfisher, 2004)
"Are you an ant? If you are, your mother is a queen..." Books in this delightful series let children view the world from an insect's point of view.

Flit, Flutter, Fly! Poems About Bugs and Other Crawly Creatures selected by Lee Bennett Hopkins (Doubleday, 1992)
Playful poems invite children into the enchanting world of butterflies, bumblebees, and other favorite "crawly creatures."

The Icky Bug Alphabet Book by Jerry Pallotta (Charlesbridge, 1987)
From ants to zebra butterflies, this book brings the world of insects and bugs to life with fun, informative facts and bold illustrations.

Insects **(National Audubon Society First Field Guides)** by Christina Wilsdon, Annette Tison, Talus Taylor (Scholastic, 1998)
Just the right size to pack in a pocket or backpack, this guide will inspire young entomologists with its vivid photographs and detailed text.

Web Site

Class Insecta
www.insecta.com
Look up the insect of the month and learn its proper name, size, and geographic location. Find out when you can see it and what sounds it makes. Interesting facts are included—for example, ladybugs' bright colors give birds a warning that they don't taste good!

Materials

- newspaper
- white bulletin board paper
- tempera paints (assorted colors)
- shallow paint containers (paper plates, bowls, or styrofoam trays)
- paintbrushes
- plastic combs with wide teeth

Sky and Grass

1. Cover a work area on the floor with newspaper. On the floor, spread out paper cut to fit your bulletin board or display area. Provide tempera paints in containers (blue and white for sky, green and yellow for grass) and paintbrushes.

2. Invite children to experiment with mixing colors to create different shades—for example, blue mixed with white makes a light sky blue and adding yellow to green makes light green for grass. (Remind children to use a fresh brush for each new color.)

3. While the paint is still wet, show children how to drag plastic combs vertically through the light green paint, creating a grass texture. Let the paint dry.

Materials

- tempera paints (assorted colors)
- shallow paint containers (paper plates, bowls, or styrofoam trays)
- paintbrushes
- strips of corrugated cardboard, cut into assorted lengths
- plastic bags

Flowers and Earth

1. Continue to work on the floor. Spread out the sky and grass background. Provide a variety of tempera paints in containers (green, black, brown, white, red, orange, yellow, and purple), paintbrushes, strips of corrugated cardboard in different sizes, and plastic bags.

2. Demonstrate how to paint the edge of a corrugated cardboard strip with green paint and use it to print a flower stem in the grass area. Then continue printing flower stems.

3. Show children how to crumple up a plastic bag, dip it into a bright color, and make a print at the top of the stem, creating a flower blossom. Use a different plastic bag for each tray of color to keep colors pure.

4. For earth, let children dip plastic bags into black, brown, and white paint and then stamp earthlike textures at the bottom of the paper. Let the paint dry.

Insects

1. Review the characteristics of an insect (*three body parts, six legs; some types have wings and antennae.*)

2. Divide the class into small groups. Provide each group with tissue and construction paper, cellophane, pipe cleaners, pom-poms, craft sticks, wiggle eyes, scissors, glue, and tape.

3. Invite children to assemble their own incredible insect using the materials provided. Remind them that their creatures should have the basic attributes of an insect.

Materials ————

- **tissue paper, construction paper, cellophane, pipe cleaners, pom-poms, craft sticks, wiggle eyes, and other craft materials**
- **scissors**
- **glue**
- **tape**

To Assemble

1. Work as a class to assemble the garden insect world. Staple the painted background paper to the bulletin board.

2. Stretch and staple cotton balls to create clouds in the sky.

3. Staple dried cornhusks or raffia to the grass area for a three-dimensional effect.

4. Attach the insects to the garden, stapling them to appropriate sections. For example, an ant might be found crawling in the earth and a dragonfly fluttering in the sky. What kinds of insects might be near the grass and flowers? (*Bees and butterflies are two examples.*)

Materials ————

- **stapler**
- **cotton balls**
- **dried cornhusks or raffia (available in craft stores)**

Writing Connection: Alliteration List Poem

1. Together with your students, stand back and admire your insect garden. Then ask children to identify the types of insects they see as well as other elements in the garden.

2. On chart paper, write "In Our Garden We Have . . . , " and then challenge children to describe their insects using words that begin with the same sound as their critters (alliteration)—for example, *little ladybugs, beautiful butterflies, active ants,* or *dazzling dragonflies.*

3. Record children's responses on the chart paper to make a collaborative list poem. Then invite visitors to your classroom and host a poetry reading!

Materials ————

- **chart paper**
- **marker**

In Our Garden We Have . . .

Lovely ladybugs	Green grass
Beautiful butterflies	Cute caterpillars
Bright blossoms	Amazing ants
Buzzing bumblebees	

by Room 101

Life in a Tide Pool

Bring the inhabitants of a tide pool into your classroom with this colorful 3-D wall display. Then invite children to use the sights, sounds, smells, and textures of this habitat as a basis for creating sensory-rich images in writing.

Book Links

Along the Seashore by Ann Cooper
(Roberts Rinehart, 1997)
Part of the Wild Wonders series, this book explores hermit crabs and other inhabitants of the North American Pacific shoreline.

Look Closer: Tide Pool
by Frank Greenaway and Christiane Gunzi
(Dorling Kindersley, 1992)
Get a close-up look at a sea urchin's spines and learn how a sea anemone eats, in this book filled with photographs that bring tide pools to life.

What's in the Tide Pool? by Anne Hunter
(Houghton Mifflin, 2000)
Charming illustrations and informative text introduce readers to periwinkles, sea anemones, hermit crabs, blue mussels, barnacles, and other tide pool creatures.

Web Site

Life at the Edge of the Sea: Virtual Tide Pool
www.pbs.org/wnet/nature/edgeofsea/tidepool.html
This interactive page from the PBS series *Nature* invites viewers to take a close-up look at the plants and animals that live in an actual tide pool.

Getting Started

1. Prepare children for this project by reading and learning about life in a tide pool. Share some of the titles in Books Links, or vist the suggested Web site, left. (Always supervise children's use of the Internet.) Then ask children questions, such as "What tide pool creature do you find most interesting? Why?" Also discuss the special adaptations these hardy animals have for surviving in such a harsh environment. (*For example, barnacles produce a superstrong cement that helps them stick to rocks despite crashing ocean waves; sea urchins have sharp spines to keep them safe from predators.*)

2. Tell children that they will use what they have learned to create a tide pool—and the creatures that live in it—right in the classroom.

Tide Pool Background

1. Cover a work area on the floor with newspaper. Then spread out paper large enough to fit your bulletin board.

2. Lightly pencil the paper into three horizontal sections: spray zone, ocean, and sand.

3. Create the spray zone (the area where only the spray of the ocean reaches): Provide blue tempera paint in containers and old toothbrushes. Demonstrate how to dip a toothbrush in blue paint and then stroke a thumb over the brush to release the paint on the paper and splatter ocean spray in the sky.

4. Beneath the ocean spray, have children paint a blue ocean section.

5. Beneath the ocean area, use a scrap of cardboard to evenly apply glue across the surface of the paper. Then have children sprinkle cornmeal over the glue to simulate sand. Let the paint dry.

6. Invite children to work in small groups to create a few each of different tide pool creatures. Select from the creatures that follow.

Materials ———

- newspaper
- white bulletin board paper
- pencil
- blue tempera paint
- shallow paint container (paper plate, bowl, or styrofoam tray)
- old toothbrushes (see note on page 5)
- paintbrushes
- cardboard scraps
- cornmeal
- glue

Sea Urchins

1. Cover work surfaces with newspaper. Provide children with styrofoam balls (cut in half), toothpicks, a large bowl half-filled with purple paint, and plastic forks.

2. Have children break toothpicks in half, then stick the broken ends into a styrofoam dome, repeating until the dome surface is mostly covered. (Explain that these represent the sea urchin's spines, which help the creature move, keep it safe from predators, and trap food.)

3. Show children how to stick the prongs of a fork into the flat side of the styrofoam dome to make a handle. Set out purple paint. Then, holding the fork handle, direct children to dip the prickly side of the dome into the paint, coating the toothpicks and the styrofoam. Let excess paint drip off.

4. Carefully remove the forks and set the urchins dome-side down to dry.

Materials ———

- newspapers
- styrofoam balls, cut in half
- toothpicks
- purple tempera paint
- large bowl
- plastic forks

Materials ————

- newspaper
- empty bathroom tissue rolls, cut in half
- tempera paints (orange, pink, and green)
- shallow paint containers (paper plates, bowls, or styrofoam trays)
- paintbrushes
- tissue paper, cut into 4½- by 12-inch strips (orange, pink, and green)
- scissors
- glue

Materials ————

- newspaper
- cardboard egg cartons
- tempera paints (white, black, and brown)
- shallow paint containers (paper plates, bowls, or styrofoam trays)
- paintbrushes
- scissors
- pencils
- white craft feathers

Sea Anemones

1. Cover work surfaces with newspaper. Provide children with the bathroom tissue rolls, tempera paints in containers, and paintbrushes.

2. Let children choose a color to paint the inside and outside of a paper roll. Let the paint dry.

3. Provide scissors, glue, and a supply of tissue paper strips. Tell children to choose a strip in the same color as their painted roll. Show them how to wrap the tissue paper around the roll and glue in place.

4. Next, model how to fringe the excess tissue paper by cutting parallel slits about ¼-inch apart. (Explain that these represent the anemone's feeding tentacles, which sweep into the mouth of this creature that attaches itself to rocks and stays in one place.)

5. Vary the size of the anemones by cutting the bottom of the rolls to different lengths.

Barnacles

1. Cover work surfaces with newspaper. Provide children with egg cartons, tempera paints in containers, and paintbrushes.

2. Show children how to cut the egg cartons into individual egg cups.

3. Have children use white, black, and brown paint to mix light gray or tan and then brush the mixed color on the outside of an egg cup. Set the egg cups upside down and let the paint dry.

4. Help children use a pencil point to poke a tiny hole in the bottom of each egg cup. Then have them insert a white feather in the hole. (Explain that the barbs of the feather represent the barnacle's feathery feet, which, like the anemone's tentacles, serve to catch food for this creature that stays in one place.)

Sea Stars

1. Supply sea star templates, coarse sandpaper, scissors, and crayons in an assortment of colors.

2. Have children trace and cut out the sea star templates from the sandpaper.

3. Using crayons, children can make designs on the rough sandpaper surface of their sea stars.

Materials ━━━━━━

- **sea star template, page 16**
- **coarse sandpaper**
- **scissors**
- **crayons (assorted colors)**

Limpids

1. Cover work surfaces with newspaper. Provide children with white construction paper, juice can lids, pencils, and scissors.

2. Have children trace the lids onto the construction paper and then cut out the circles.

3. Provide tempera paints in containers and paintbrushes. Invite children to mix light colors, such as lavender, gray, and tan.

Materials ━━━━━━

- **newspaper**
- **white construction paper**
- **juice can lids with smooth edges**
- **pencils**
- **scissors**
- **tempera paints (white, purple, black, and brown)**
- **paint containers (paper plates, bowls, or styrofoam trays)**
- **paintbrushes**
- **old toothbrushes (See note on page 5.)**
- **black markers**
- **stapler**

4. Demonstrate how to splatter paint onto the limpid circles: Dip an old toothbrush in paint, then stroke a thumb over the brush to splatter paint on the circle. Encourage children to experiment with different paints to build up the surface color. Allow drying time.

5. Model how to use a black marker to draw lines, like the spokes on a wheel, outward from the center of the circle.

6. Show children how to cut a slit in the circle, stopping at the center.

7. To create a domed peak, have them overlap the cut edges slightly, then staple closed.

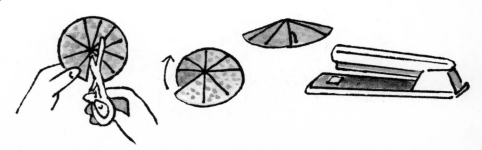

Materials ————

- mussel template, page 16
- 4½- by 12-inch pieces of black construction paper
- pencils
- scissors
- light pink tissue paper
- glue

————

Materials ——————

- 6-inch paper plates
- scissors
- newspaper
- crab templates, page 16
- pencils
- tempera paints (brown and white)
- paintbrushes
- shallow paint containers (paper plates, bowls, or styrofoam trays)
- brown paper bags
- stapler
- black pipe cleaners, cut in half
- tape

——————

Mussels

1. Provide children with copies of the mussel template, black construction paper, pencils, and scissors.

2. Instruct children to fold a piece of construction paper in half. Then demonstrate how to position the template on the fold and then trace and cut out the shape to create the two sides of a mussel shell.

fold

3. Let children crumple pieces of light-pink tissue paper into a ball, and then glue in place between the two halves of the mussel shell. (Explain that the tissue paper ball represents the mussel.)

Crabs

1. Ahead of time, make crab bodies from paper plates by cutting out curved sections, as shown.

2. Cover work surfaces with newspaper. Provide children with the paper plate crab bodies, paints in containers, and paintbrushes. Let children mix light brown to paint the convex (bulging) side of the crab's body. Let the paint dry.

3. Give children the front claw and leg templates and paper bags. Show them how to position the templates on the bag and then trace and cut out the shapes.

4. Direct children to position the front claws and back legs under the crab's body, and then staple to secure.

5. For eyes, have children use a pencil point to poke two holes near the front of the crab. Then direct them to thread each end of a black pipe cleaner from the underside of the crab up through the holes. A piece of tape will secure the pipe cleaner to the bottom of the crab. Then they can twist the tips of each pipe cleaner stalk to create eyes.

Seagulls

1. Supply children with the seagull template, construction paper, pencils, and scissors.

2. Direct children to fold a piece of construction paper in half. Demonstrate how to position the template on the fold, trace it, and then cut out the shape. Children can then open up the folded paper to see the entire bird.

Materials ━ ━ ━ ━ ━

- seagull template, page 16
- blue, gray, or white 9- by 12-inch sheets of construction paper
- pencils
- scissors

━ ━ ━ ━ ━ ━ ━ ━ ━ ━

To Assemble

1. Work as a class to assemble the tide pool. Staple the background to the bulletin board.

2. Create rocks by crumbling pieces of brown paper bags. Then arrange them around the water area, and staple to secure them in place.

3. Staple the seagulls in the sky.

4. Add the rest of the creatures to the scene. (Cluster the mussels in groups, attach the barnacles to the rocks, place the sea anemones in the water areas between the rocks, and so on.)

Materials ━ ━ ━ ━ ━

- stapler
- brown paper bag

━ ━ ━ ━ ━ ━ ━ ━ ━ ━

Writing Connection:
Using Sensory Descriptions

Invite children to imagine they are at their tide pool. What can they see, hear, smell, and feel? On chart paper, make a four-column chart, one for each of these senses. Record in the corresponding column descriptive words about the creatures and setting that children volunteer—for example, *hard shells, salty sea air, rough rocks, sharp crab claws*.

Materials ━ ━ ━ ━ ━

- chart paper
- markers

━ ━ ━ ━ ━ ━ ━ ━ ━ ━

SEE	HEAR	SMELL	FEEL
purple sea urchins black mussels bright anemones	seagulls cry waves crash wind whistles	salty sea air fresh breeze	sharp crab claws spiky urchins hard shells of mussels rough rocks

Life in a Tide Pool Templates

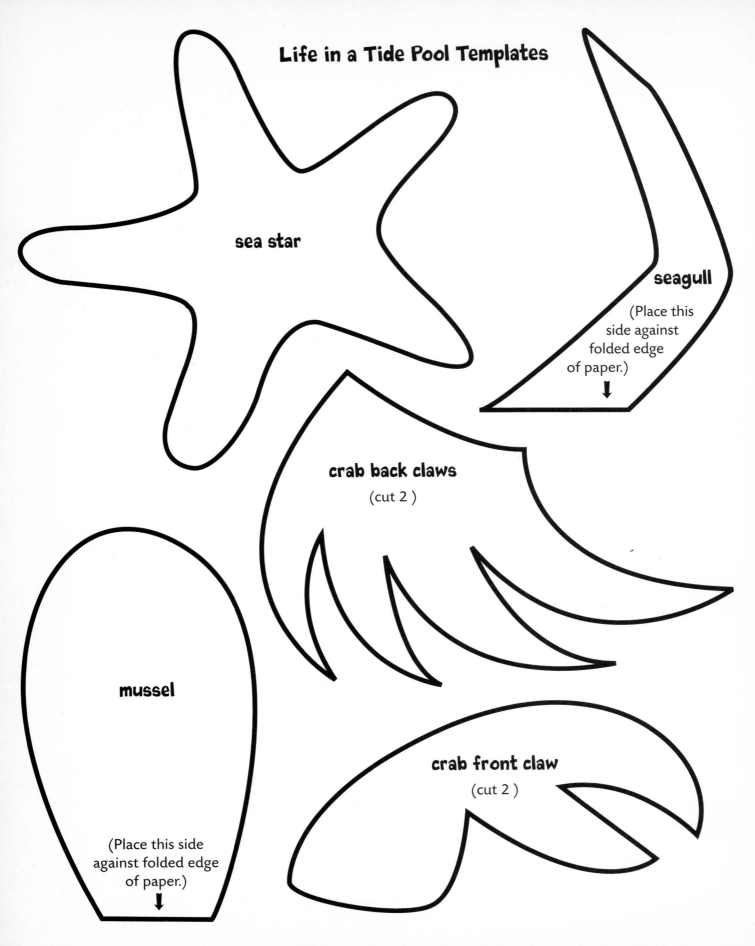

sea star

seagull

(Place this side against folded edge of paper.)

crab back claws

(cut 2)

mussel

crab front claw

(cut 2)

(Place this side against folded edge of paper.)

Collaborative Art & Writing Projects for Young Learners Scholastic Teaching Resources

Underwater World

How are the creatures of the sea adapted for life in the ocean? In this project, children learn about creatures that live in the sea and the features that help them get around in their underwater world. Two- and three-dimensional sea creatures combine to make this an exciting display.

Getting Started

I. Invite children to explore the variety of creatures that live in the ocean. Share some of the titles in Book Links, or visit the suggested Web site, right. (Always supervise children's use of the Internet.) Encourage children to notice the features that help different ocean animals move—for example, fish use fins and tails; jellyfish propel themselves by rhythmically pulsing their bell-shaped bodies; the octopus uses its long arms to crawl along the ocean floor and also to swim.

2. Invite children to describe the many shapes, colors, patterns, sizes, and other features of fish.

3. Tell children to get ready to create a colorful and exciting underwater world on a wall of your classroom.

Book Links

Alphabet Sea by Carolyn Spencer (Tortuga Books, 1999)
Rhyming text and color photographs introduce the ABCs of sea life.

Dear Fish by Chris Gall (Little, Brown, 2006)
"Dear Fish: Where you live is pretty cool. You should visit us someday..." A boy visiting the seashore sends a letter to the fish, and silliness ensues when they take him up on his offer to visit. The fish in the story are identified in informative endpapers.

Down, Down, Down in the Ocean by Sandra Markle (Walker, 1999)
The four layers of the ocean—surface, twilight, bottom, and seafloor—all come alive with informative text and striking illustrations.

Exploring the Deep, Dark Sea by Gail Gibbons (Little, Brown, 1999)
Dive in and follow a submersible 7,500 feet down to the ocean floor to see what lives at each level. A time line provides additional support for reading nonfiction.

Web Site

Monterey Bay Aquarium
www.mbayaq.org
Watch videos of dancing jellyfish, a giant octopus, sharks, sea turtles, and other creatures on live Web cams, and learn more from an online field guide and dictionary at this award-winning Web site.

Materials

- white bulletin board paper
- shallow containers, such as styrofoam trays
- dish soap
- food coloring (blues and greens)
- bubble-blowing rings
- plastic forks or plastic combs with wide teeth
- jumbo pasta shells
- glue

Ocean Background

1. On a nice day, go outside with your class and spread out paper precut to fit your bulletin board or display area.

2. In the shallow containers, mix equal parts dish soap, water, and food coloring. Provide bubble-blowing rings, shallow trays, and forks or combs.

3. Have children take turns dipping the bubble-blowing rings into the colored soap and blowing bubbles onto the paper.

4. Pour excess colored soap into shallow trays. Show children how to dip the combs or forks into the colored soap and drag wavy lines across the paper.

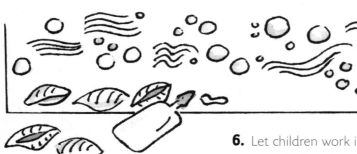

5. Provide jumbo pasta shells and glue. Direct children to dip the pasta shells in glue and then position them along the bottom of the paper to suggest shells on the ocean floor. Let the paint dry.

6. Let children work in small groups to create a few each of different ocean animals described below and on page 19.

Materials

- construction paper (assorted colors)
- decorative papers (foil, patterned papers)
- scissors
- glue and glue sticks
- glitter, sequins, stickers, and other decorating materials

Fish

1. Supply construction paper in assorted colors, scissors, glue and glue sticks, and markers or crayons.

2. Tell children to tear or cut construction paper to create imaginary or realistic fish.

3. Encourage children to think about the features that make fish unique, such as body parts like eyes, gills, fins, and tails, as well as other distinguishing characteristics, such as colors, patterns, and so on. Invite children to cut or tear paper scraps to add these features to their fish. They can also use glitter, sequins, stickers, and other decorating materials.

Octopus

1. Provide students with brown paper lunch bags, paper towels, and rubber bands.

2. Crumple paper towels and stuff them into the bottom of a lunch bag. Show children how to create a round form by tucking in the corners of the bag. Wrap a rubber band around this section of the bag to define the head of the octopus.

Materials ————

- **brown paper lunch bags**
- **paper towels**
- **rubber bands**
- **scissors**
- **O-shaped cereal**
- **glue**

3. Ask students if they know how many arms an octopus has (*eight*). Use scissors to demonstrate how to cut the remainder of the bag into eight sections to make the arms of the octopus.

4. Provide O-shaped cereal and glue. Tell children to glue pieces of O-shaped cereal along each of the arms. These represent the suction cups that help an octopus hold on to rocks and also to taste its food.

Jellyfish

1. Provide students with tissue paper in assorted colors, pieces of clear cellophane, tape, and scissors.

Materials ————

- **tissue paper (assorted colors)**
- **pieces of clear cellophane, approximately 24 by 30 inches**
- **tape**
- **scissors**

2. Demonstrate how to crumple a piece of colored tissue paper into a ball. Then wrap a piece of cellophane several times around the tissue paper ball to create an iridescent jelly body. Secure the cellophane-covered ball with clear tape.

3. Instruct children to cut long, thin strips of cellophane and tape them to the body to make jellyfish tentacles. The tentacles help jellyfish bring food to their mouths, which are on the underside of their bodies.

Materials

- green crepe paper streamers
- stapler

To Assemble

1. Work as a class to assemble your underwater world. Staple the ocean background to the bulletin board.

2. To add seaweed that appears to be gently moving in the ocean, staple the ends of green crepe paper streamers along the bottom of the scene. Twist each strand loosely, and then staple the other end of the streamer near the top of the scene. Position the seaweed to avoid covering the shells.

3. Position and staple fish, octopuses, and jellyfish throughout the ocean scene.

Materials

- 5- by 8-inch unlined index cards
- markers

Writing Connection: Using Vivid Verbs

1. What goes on under the sea? Ask children to think of action words that specifically describe the movements of different ocean creatures—for example, fish might *glide, drift, wiggle, zip, loop, spin, dive, dart,* or *dip* to get around. Octopuses or jellyfish might use their arms and tentacles to *wave, sway,* or *push* through the water.

2. Provide index cards and ask children to select an underwater creature to write or dictate an action phrase about. Staple the phrase cards to the display to create a collaborative poem. Invite children to take turns reading and acting out their contributions.

Tiny fish zip and dart, escaping the waving octopus.

Jellies glide by gracefully. Drifting along they go.

Eight arms reach, grab, and suck. Watch out!

Fish dance together like a ballet class. They spin and loop, dip, and wiggle.

Seaweed sways.

Bubbles burst as fish speed by.

Neighborhood Walk

Build a neighborhood in your classroom with this collaborative panel collage. The diverse buildings, people, and activities portrayed will inspire young writers to rich explorations of point of view.

Getting Started

1. Launch your study of the neighborhood by giving children clipboards, paper, and pencils and taking your class on a neighborhood walk. Encourage children to draw sketches and take notes about the kinds of buildings they see.

2. Back in the classroom, ask children to name some of the places they saw—for example, a grocery school, post office, bank, and library. Encourage them to share their sketches and describe how the places are different from one another and ways they might be alike. To help children learn more about ways people use the different buildings they observed, share some of the resources suggested in Book Links, right.

3. If possible, also share Romare Bearden's work *The Block*, a tribute to his old neighborhood, Harlem. Invite children to describe the details they see in his artwork. How did the artist create this work? Discuss his collage technique and the materials he might have used. Then tell children that they are going to create a collage of a block in their neighborhood.

Book Links

The Block by Langston Hughes
(Viking/Metropolitan Museum of Art, 1995)
Poems by Langston Hughes are paired with Romare Bearden's impressive collage tribute to Harlem.

Cassi's Word Quilt by Faith Ringgold (Knopf, 2002)
A young African-American girl takes early readers on a tour of her 1930s Harlem home, school, and neighborhood.

One Afternoon by Yumi Heo (Orchard Books, 1994)
Minho, a Korean-American boy, joins his mother on her daily errands. Together, they encounter the many sights and sounds of life in New York City.

On the Town: A Community Adventure by Judith Caseley (Greenwillow, 2002)
As Charlie and his mother explore their community, Charlie's lively notebook entries "illustrate" their adventure.

A Street Called Home by Aminah Brenda Lynn Robinson (Harcourt, 1997)
Children will want to stretch out this accordion-fold book and immerse themselves in the stunning streetscape, where they'll meet the sock man, the medicine man, the chickenfoot woman, and other people in this busy 1940s community.

Uptown by Bryan Collier
(Henry Holt, 2000)
A young boy takes readers on a tour that celebrates his vibrant Harlem community. Richly illustrated in watercolor and collage.

Materials

- **tagboard (cut into pieces 9, 15, and 18 inches high by 12 inches wide)**
- **ruler**
- **construction paper, corrugated bordette, foil, and other decorative papers**
- **cardboard scraps**
- **fabric trim (rickrack, lace, braid, yarn)**
- **craft sticks**
- **craft foam**
- **cellophane (assorted colors)**
- **magazines, catalogs, and newspapers (with pictures of people, trees, buildings, transportation vehicles, signs, textures, and more)**
- **scissors**
- **tempera paints**
- **paint containers (paper plates, bowls, or styrofoam trays)**
- **paintbrushes**
- **markers**
- **pencils**
- **glue**

Building Panels

1. Precut tagboard panels in three different heights (to create an interesting roofline) but in a uniform width (to allow accordion assembling).

2. Rule off four inches along the bottom of each panel. This portion will be reserved for children's writings about their buildings, and will also function as the street.

4"

3. Divide the class into small groups. Provide each group with assorted papers, cardboard scraps, fabric trim, craft sticks, craft foam, colored cellophane, magazines, catalogs, and newspapers, scissors, tempera paints in containers, paintbrushes, markers, pencils, and glue. Also give each child a tagboard panel.

4. Ask each child to choose a building in the neighborhood to create. Children can then work on a single panel—drawing, painting, and combining collage elements and magazine and newspaper pictures to portray their building. Encourage children to think about what makes their building unique by asking questions:

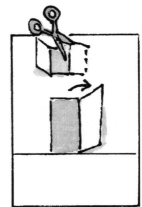

- "What size is your building? Is it tall? Short?"
- "What shape roof does it have?"
- "Does it have windows and doors? If so, how many?" (Children can make windows and doors by cutting flaps in the tagboard, folding them back, and then gluing photos or drawings of interior scenes to the back of the panel. The doors and windows can then be closed and opened to reveal what's going on inside.)
- "Does your building have a sign? If so, what does the sign say?"

5. Invite children to add transportation vehicles, trees, traffic signals, people, and other details on the street below their building.

Writing Connection: Exploring Point of View

Materials ━━━━━━
- white paper
- pencils
- thin markers
- glue

━ ━ ━ ━ ━ ━ ━ ━ ━

Ask each child to describe his or her building and the reasons people go to each place. Tell children to use the first-person ("I") voice and write a brief story from the point of view of their building or a character in their panel. Have them work on separate paper, and then copy and glue a finished, revised story to the bottom section of the panel.

> I am the school building. My halls are crazy crowded one minute. When everyone goes in a different door, my halls are silent. I have friends during the day, but I am lonely at night.

To Assemble

Materials ━━━━━━
- tape

━ ━ ━ ━ ━ ━ ━ ━ ━

1. Assemble the neighborhood by turning the building panels facedown, aligning them side by side, and then hinging them together with tape. Instant neighborhood!

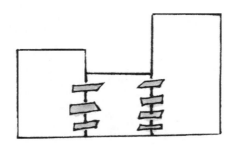

2. Display your neighborhood collage on a bulletin board or tabletop and let children lead tours, introducing the many voices of the neighborhood.

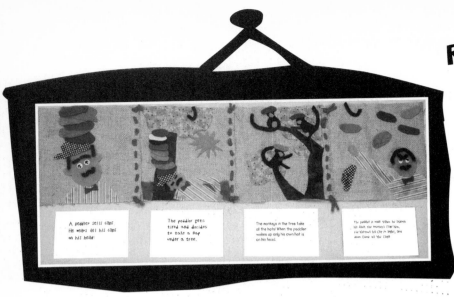

Retell a Story Cloth

In some cultures, people tell stories through picture collages made with textiles. This story cloth project is a fun way to help children practice retelling a favorite tale.

Book Links

Caps for Sale by Esphyr Slobodkina
(Harper & Row, 1947)
In this best-loved classic, mischievous monkeys play tricks on a peddler who sells colorful caps.

The Enormous Turnip by Kathy Parkinson
(Whitman, 1985)
In this retelling of a cumulative tale, one of Grandfather's turnips grows so big that the entire family, including the pets, must try to pull it up.

The Frog and Toad Collection by Arnold Lobel
(HarperCollins, 2004)
These hilarious and heartwarming stories, including the Caldecott Honor book *Frog and Toad Are Friends* and the Newbery Honor book *Frog and Toad Together,* follow the daily adventures of two best friends.

The Mitten by Jan Brett (Putnam, 1990)
What happens when a little boy drops a mitten in the snow? One by one, forest animals crawl inside to stay warm.

Who Sank the Boat? by Pamela Allen (Putnam, 1996)
A cow, a donkey, a sheep, a pig, and a mouse decide to go rowing in a very small boat. The suspense grows as each climbs aboard and the boat comes closer to sinking.

Why Mosquitoes Buzz in People's Ears by Verna Aardema (Dial, 1975)
In this Caldecott Medal–winning adaptation of a traditional African tale, one misunderstanding leads to another between jungle animals.

Getting Started

1. Choose a piece of literature that lends itself to making a story cloth. (It's helpful to choose a story that has at least several characters and a lot of action.) For suggestions, see Book Links, left.

2. Read the story to children over the course of several days so that they become very familiar with it. Then discuss the parts of the story, asking children who the important characters are, where the story takes place, what happened first, next, and so on. On chart paper, record children's responses, dividing the story into beginning, middle, and end scenes.
   For example, a chart outlining the story *Caps for Sale* might look like this:
   - First, a cap peddler sits down under a tree to take a nap.
   - While he sleeps, a pack of monkeys each takes one of his caps.
   - The peddler is furious! The monkeys imitate the gestures of the angry peddler.
   - Finally, in anger he throws down his cap. The monkeys copy him and down come all the caps!

3. Tell children that they are going to create their own cloths to retell the story they just read.

Tip: *Divide the class into small groups and assign each group a specific scene in the story to depict.*

Story Cloth Squares

1. Provide groups with burlap squares, fabric scraps, fabric trim, yarn in assorted colors, plastic needles, glue, and scissors.

2. Demonstrate how to cut, position, and glue fabric shapes, pieces of trim, and yarn to the burlap background to create a picture. Allow glue to dry thoroughly. Older children may wish to attach fabrics and trims by sewing with plastic needles threaded with yarn.

Materials ————————

- 12-inch burlap squares
- fabric scraps (felt, patterned cottons, textured fabrics)
- fabric trim, such as rickrack and braids
- yarns in assorted colors
- large plastic needles
- glue
- scissors

To Assemble

1. Thread plastic needles with yarn and knot the ends.

2. Ask children to put the cloth squares in sequence. Then show them how to attach the cloth squares to each other by overlapping the squares and sewing through both layers of fabric. The story cloths can be organized horizontally or vertically.

Materials ————————

- large plastic needles
- yarn
- scissors

Writing Connection: Retelling a Story

1. Display the story cloth and invite children to study their creation. What characters are depicted? What is the sequence of events? What details do children notice?

Materials ————————

chart paper

markers

2. Encourage children to use the story cloth to collectively retell the story in their own words. Encourage them to use descriptive language, dialogue, and other details. Have them dictate their retelling to you as you write it on a sheet of chart paper.

3. Display the story cloth with children's written retelling pinned up nearby.

A peddler sells caps. He wears all his caps on his head!

The peddler gets tired and decides to take a nap under a tree.

The monkeys in the tree take all the hats! When the peddler wakes up only his own hat is on his head.

The peddler is mad! When he stamps his feet the monkeys copy him. He throws his cap in anger, and down come all the caps!

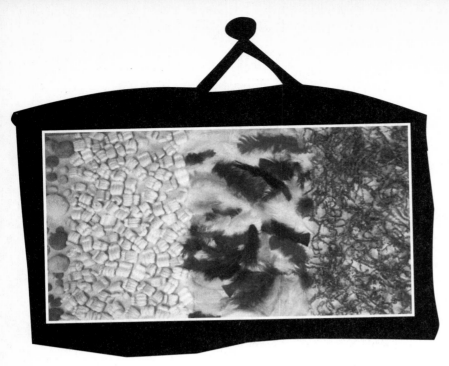

Texture Road

For this project, children will enjoy casting off their shoes, feeling different textures with their feet, and then brainstorming words to describe how the textures feel.

Book Links

Feeling Things by Allan Fowler (Children's Press, 1991)
Explore the sense of touch and how it helps tell us about the world around us.

I Can Tell by Touching by Carolyn Otto (HarperCollins, 1994)
Evocative descriptions of a child's exploration of his sense of touch are a highlight of this book.

Is It Rough? Is It Smooth? Is It Shiny? by Tana Hoban (Greenwillow, 1984)
The tree photographed for this book is rough. But what else is it? The more readers look, the more they will discover about the objects shown!

My Five Senses by Aliki (HarperTrophy, 1989)
Simple text and delightful illustrations invite young children to experience their world through sight, sound, taste, smell, and touch.

My Five Senses by Margaret Miller (Aladdin, 1998)
Predictable text and photographs of familiar experiences invite children to explore the world through their senses.

You Can't Taste a Pickle With Your Ear: A Book About Your 5 Senses by Harriet Ziebert (Handprint Books, 2002)
In this humorous book with whimsical illustrations, young readers learn about the special qualities of each of the five senses.

Getting Started

1. Before beginning this project with your class, gather objects that have contrasting shapes and textures—for example, a wooden block, an orange, a banana, a piece of sandpaper, a pompom or cotton ball, a small stuffed animal toy, a ribbon, a shell, and a feather. Place the objects in separate paper bags.

2. Invite volunteers to take turns putting a hand in the bag (without looking). Ask them to feel the object and try to guess what it is. Encourage children to use words that describe the shape of the object as well as how it feels—for example, *square, hard, long, pointy, round, bumpy, soft, fuzzy, thin, grainy, furry, rough*.

3. Start a word wall of "touch" words. You might list them in pairs of opposites (*hard/soft, bumpy/smooth,* and so on). Encourage children to continue adding words as they work on the art project.

4. Besides using their fingers to experience the sense of touch, we also use the rest of our skin to feel things. Ask children to think of other ways they feel with their skin—for example, rain on their faces or hot sand on their bare feet. Then tell children that they are going to do an art project that will let them explore different textures with their feet!

Texture Road

1. On a work area on the floor, spread a length of easel paper long enough for each child to have a 12-inch section on which to work. Use a ruler to lightly pencil 12-inch sections.

2. Set out a selection of textured materials. Also provide scissors, glue, and cardboard scraps.

3. Invite children to contribute to the project one at a time. Let each child come to the work area and choose one of the textured materials.

4. Demonstrate how to prepare the paper surface by distributing the glue with the edge of a cardboard scrap. Then have the child apply the textured material to that section of the paper. After everyone has contributed, let the glue dry completely.

Materials ━ ━ ━ ━ ━

- **easel paper on a roll (narrower than bulletin board paper)**
- **assorted textured materials (that are safe for walking on without shoes): cotton balls, plastic grass, craft feathers, sandpaper, styrofoam peanuts, pom-poms, plastic bags, bubble wrap, cornmeal, aluminum foil, dried split peas, lentils, rice, ribbon, yarn, string, and more**
- **scissors**
- **glue**
- **cardboard scraps**
- **markers**

━ ━ ━ ━ ━ ━ ━ ━ ━ ━

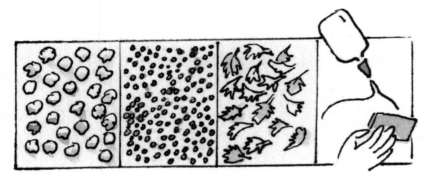

Writing Connection: Building Vocabulary

1. On a sheet of paper, create a recording sheet like the one shown here. Make a copy for each of the textures on the road. Fill in the name of each material as indicated.

2. Invite children to take turns walking barefoot over each of the textures on the road they created. As they walk, ask them to describe how each texture looks and feels. For example, feathers might be *fluffy, tickly,* and *soft;* styrofoam peanuts might be *bouncy* and *squishy;* plastic bags might be *smooth* and *slippery;* while rice might feel *grainy, bumpy, hard,* and *rough.*

3. After children have taken their walk, position the record sheets near each texture on the road. Ask children to fill in (or dictate) a word to complete the sentence frame for each material.

4. Invite children to compare and contrast the different materials and discuss their explorations and discoveries. Then add the "touch" words to your word wall.

Materials ━ ━ ━ ━ ━

- **white paper**
- **markers**

━ ━ ━ ━ ━ ━ ━ ━ ━ ━

> **We walked on** <u>pom-poms</u>.
>
> **They/It felt** <u>fluffy</u>
> <u>tickly</u>
> <u>puffy</u>.

Land of the Dinosaurs

Capture children's natural fascination with dinosaurs! Have your class re-create the prehistoric world of dinosaurs and then write what they know about these amazing creatures.

Book Links

Digging Up Dinosaurs by Alki (HarperCollins, 1988)
Inviting illustrations, easy-to-read text, and captions and dialogue balloons engage young readers as a team of experts digs up dinosaur skeletons and puts them back together.

Dinosaurs: The Biggest, Baddest, Fastest, Strongest
by Howard Zimmerman and George Olshevsky (Atheneum, 2000)
Discover a dinosaur with two-and-one-half-foot-long claws and other amazing dinosaurs in this oversized, attention-grabbing book. Pronunciation guides help young readers identify their favorite colossal creatures.

Dinosaur World by Christopher Santoro
(Random House, 1997)
This hands-on flap book includes realistic panoramas and information about where dinosaurs lived, what they ate, how they bred, and how they fought.

DK Readers: Dinosaur Dinners by Lee Davis
(Dorling Kindersley, 2000)
Here's a high-interest, visually exciting book for beginning readers, and a great teacher resource for introducing dinosaurs.

Web Site

Natural History Museum's Dino Directory
www.nhm.ac.uk/jdsml/nature-online/dino-directory//
Visit the Dino Directory to learn about 190 different dinosaurs, view a dino time line, explore interactive maps that show which dinosaurs lived in the same place at the same time, and more.

Getting Started

I. Introduce your class study of dinosaurs by encouraging children to tell what they know about these extinct creatures. Also ask them to share questions that they have about them. On chart paper, make a list of their responses. Then, to help children find the answers to their questions and learn more about dinosaurs, share some of the resources listed in Book Links as well as information on the suggested Web site, left. (Always supervise children's use of the Internet.) Encourage children to find out about the different kinds of dinosaurs, how scientists think they looked, how they lived, what the earth was like then, and more.

2. Tell children to get ready for a trip way, way back in time because they are going to create a 3-D bulletin board depicting the prehistoric world of dinosaurs.

Tip: *Divide the class into small groups. One group can work on the background, another group can make the rocks, and a third group, the palm trees. Each child can then make a dinosaur to add to the scene. Each of these elements can be done over several days or sessions.*

Prehistoric Background

1. Cover a work area on the floor with newspaper. Spread out white paper cut to fit the bulletin board or display area. Provide blue, green, and brown paint in containers, paintbrushes, and paper towels.

2. Have children paint grass, land, water, mountains, and sky. Let the paint dry.

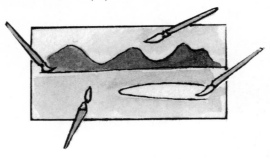

Materials ————

- newspaper
- white bulletin board paper
- tempera paints (blue, green, and brown)
- shallow paint containers (paper plates, bowls, or styrofoam trays)
- paintbrushes
- paper towels

Rocks

1. Cover a work area on the floor with newspaper. Provide additional newspaper or newsprint; black, white, and brown paints; shallow containers; brushes for mixing colors, sponges for printing; and paper towels.

2. Have children mix paints to create gray and light brown in the shallow trays.

3. Show children how to dab sponges into the mixed paints and print on the paper, covering the page. Hang or store on a flat surface to dry.

Materials ————

- newspaper or newsprint
- white paper
- tempera paints (black, white, and brown)
- paint containers (paper plates, bowls, or styrofoam trays)
- paintbrushes
- sponges
- paper towels

Palm Trees

1. Cover a work area on the floor with newspaper. Provide additional newspaper or newsprint, green paint in containers, paintbrushes, and paper towels.

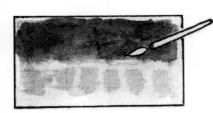

2. Have children position sheets of newspaper or newsprint horizontally and then paint the top half green. Store on a flat surface to dry.

3. To assemble the palm trees, provide children with the green-painted newspapers, scissors, tape, brown paint in containers, and paintbrushes.

Materials ————

- newspaper or newsprint
- tempera paints (green and brown)
- paint containers (paper plates, bowls, or styrofoam trays)
- paintbrushes
- paper towels
- scissors
- tape

4. Demonstrate how to make newspaper palm trees:

- Overlap and align three painted sheets of paper (painted side up).

- Roll up tightly and then tape the bottom half of the roll together.

- Make four cuts through the top half of the roll as shown.

- Poke a finger inside the top of the roll to pull out the palm tree leaves.

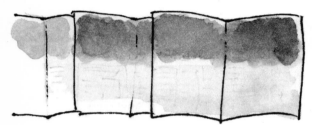 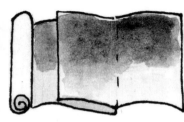 

5. Have children paint the bottom half of the palm trees brown. Let the paint dry.

Materials ----------

- **dinosaur templates, pages 32–35**
- **9- by 12-inch pieces of printed fabrics (animal prints and geometric patterns work especially well)**
- **straight pins**
- **scissors**
- **plastic sewing needles with large eyes**
- **18-inch lengths of yarn**
- **cotton balls or tissues**
- **wiggle eyes**
- **glue**

Tip: *To simplify the project, cut dinosaur patterns from paper instead of fabric. Have children paint the patterns. After the paint dries, have them align the front and back and staple closed almost all the way around the edges. Children can then stuff the dinosaurs with crumpled tissues and staple completely closed.*

Dinosaurs

1. Ahead of time, photocopy and cut out the dinosaur templates. For each dinosaur, fold a fabric square in half. Pin a template through both layers of fabric, and then cut through the two layers to create a front and back. Also thread 18-inch lengths of colored yarn through the plastic needles, double, and knot the end of the yarn.

2. Divide the class into small groups. Provide each group with a selection of precut fabric dinosaurs (fronts and backs), prethreaded needles, extra yarn, scissors, tissues, wiggle eyes, and glue.

3. Aligning the front and back pieces of cloth, demonstrate overcast stitching around the edge of the dinosaur: Push the needle through the edge of the top layer of fabric and then pull it out through the bottom layer. Repeat this over and over, moving the needle along the edge of the dinosaur.

4. Before the front and back are joined completely, show children how to fill the dinosaur with crumpled tissues.

5. Work with children individually to show them how to secure the remaining yarn and thread, and knot a new strand, if needed.

6. Invite the children to glue wiggle eyes to their completed dinosaur.

Writing Connection: Dinosaur Comparison Chart

Review the different dinosaurs children created using the templates provided as well as any others they may have chosen to make. Then ask children what they know about each type. Encourage them to refer to their resources about dinosaurs to take notes about their size, weight, what they ate, and so on. Then help children compile the information they gather on a comparison chart such as the one below.

Materials
- paper
- pencils
- chart paper
- markers

Dinosaur Comparison Chart				
Name	Measured	What It Ate	Walked On	Other Facts
Brachiosaurus	15 feet long	plants	4 legs	• weighed as much as 15 elephants • used its tail like a whip against attackers
Pterodactylus	3 feet wide (wingspan)	fish	2 legs	• had wings and could fly • caught fish with its beak • They were really flying reptiles, not dinosaurs.
Stegosaurus	30 feet long	plants	4 legs	• Its brain was smaller than a walnut. • spiky plates were for protection
Tyrannosaurus	40 feet long	meat	2 legs	• jaws could be 4 feet long • had teeth as long as steak knives

To Assemble

1. Staple the background scenery to the bulletin board.

2. Demonstrate for children how to crumple the sponge-printed papers to form rock shapes. Staple the rocks to the bulletin board scenery.

3. Staple the palm trees to the background scenery.

4. Staple the dinosaurs into their new home.

5. Post the Dinosaur Comparison Chart near the bulletin board and invite children to admire the spectacular prehistoric world they created. You might also invite visitors to your classroom and let children give tours, sharing all that they learned about these creatures.

Materials
- tape
- stapler

Land of the Dinosaurs Templates

Brachiosaurus

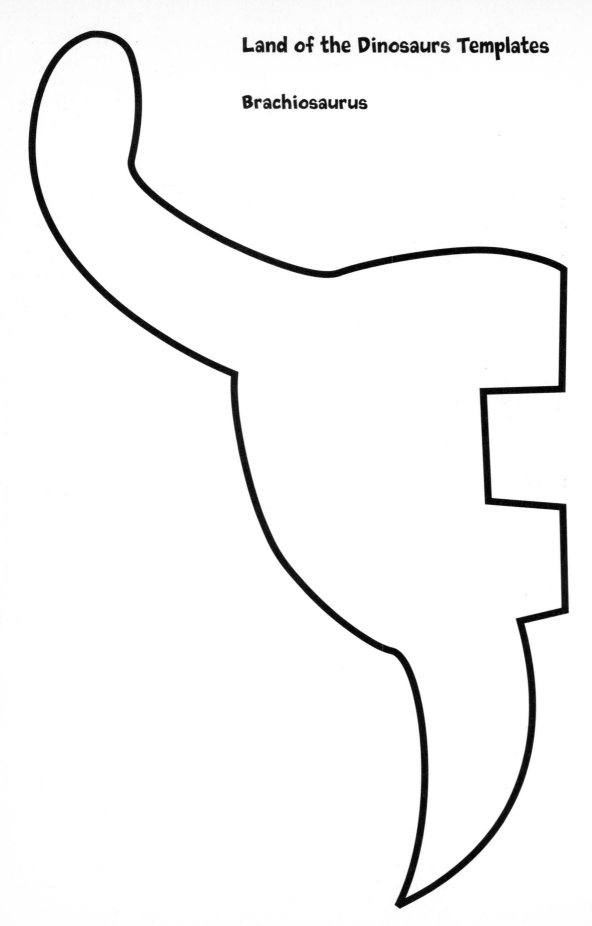

Continued on page 33

Collaborative Art & Writing Projects for Young Learners Scholastic Teaching Resources

In Our Garden We Have . . .

Lovely ladybugs	Green grass
Beautiful butterflies	Cute caterpillars
Bright blossoms	Amazing ants
Buzzing bumblebees	

by Room 101

Incredible Insects, Pages 7–9

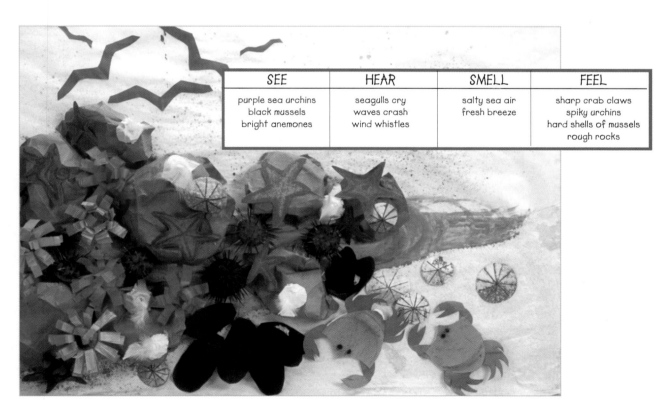

SEE	HEAR	SMELL	FEEL
purple sea urchins	seagulls cry	salty sea air	sharp crab claws
black mussels	waves crash	fresh breeze	spiky urchins
bright anemones	wind whistles		hard shells of mussels
			rough rocks

Life in a Tide Pool, Pages 10–16

Tiny fish zip and dart, escaping the waving octopus.

Jellies glide by gracefully. Drifting along they go.

Fish dance together like a ballet class. They spin and loop, dip, and wiggle.

Seaweed sways.

Eight arms reach, grab, and suck. watch out!

Bubbles burst as fish speed by.

Underwater World, Pages 17–20

Neighborhood Walk, Pages 21–23

A peddler sells caps. He wears all his caps on his head!

The peddler gets tired and decides to take a nap under a tree.

The monkeys in the tree take all the hats! When the peddler wakes up only his own hat is on his head.

The peddler is mad! When he stamps his feet the monkeys copy him. He throws his cap in anger, and down come all the caps!

Retell a Story Cloth, Pages 24–25

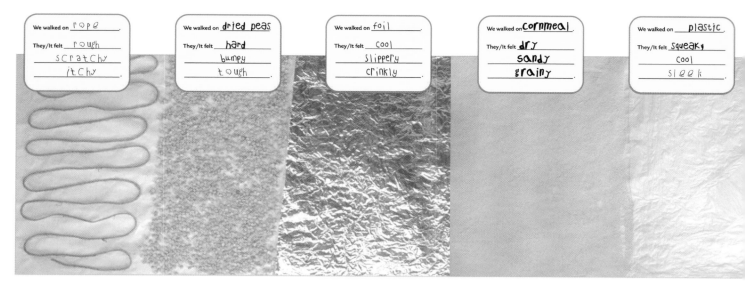

We walked on rope .

They/It felt rough
scratchy
itchy .

We walked on dried peas .

They/It felt hard
bumpy
tough .

We walked on foil .

They/It felt cool
slippery
crinkly .

We walked on cornmeal .

They/It felt dry
sandy
grainy .

We walked on plastic .

They/It felt squeaky
cool
sleek .

Texture Road, Pages 26–27

Dinosaur Comparison Chart				
Name	Measured	What It Ate	Walked On	Other Facts
Brachiosaurus	75 feet long	plants	4 legs	• weighed as much as 15 elephants • used its tail like a whip against attackers
Pterodactylus	3 feet wide (wingspan)	fish	2 legs	• had wings and could fly • caught fish with its beak • They were really flying reptiles, not dinosaurs.
Stegosaurus	30 feet long	plants	4 legs	• Its brain was smaller than a walnut. • spiky plates were for protection
Tyrannosaurus	40 feet long	meat	2 legs	• jaws could be 4 feet long • had teeth as long as steak knives

Land of the Dinosaurs, Pages 28–35

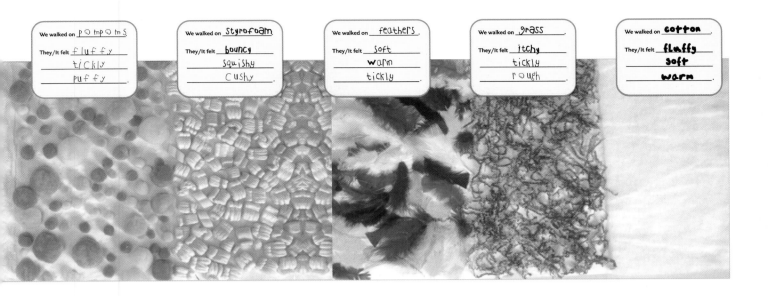

We walked on POmPOmS.
They/It felt fluffy
tickly
puffy.

We walked on Styrofoam.
They/It felt bouncy
squishy
cushy.

We walked on feathers.
They/It felt soft
warm
tickly.

We walked on grass.
They/It felt itchy
tickly
rough.

We walked on cotton.
They/It felt fluffy
soft
warm.

Name: Ben
Animal: Giraffe
Home: Africa
Habitat description:
Savanna

Name: Megha
Animal: Elephant
Home: Asia
Habitat description:
forest, grassy plains

Name: Mei
Animal: Monkey
Home: Asia
Habitat description:
mountain forest

Name: Jamal
Animal: Kangaroo
Home: Australia
Habitat description:
Hot and dry

Name: Carmen
Animal: Penguin
Home: Antarctica
Habitat description:
Cold and wet

Animals Around the World, Pages 36–38

Readable Railroad, Pages 39–41

What Grows on a Farm?, Pages 42–47

Water Cycle Go-Round, Pages 48–50

Perky Penguins, Pages 51–54

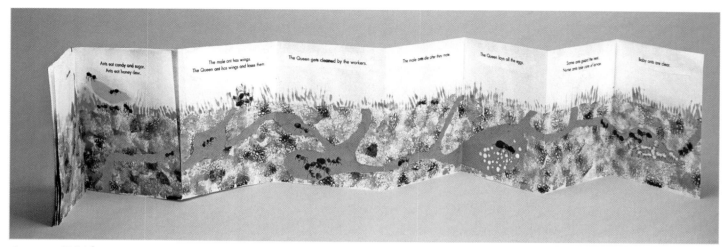

Ants at Work, Pages 55–58

Busy Bees, Pages 59–62

Butterfly Frieze, Pages 63–64

Land of the Dinosaurs Templates

Stegosaurus

Land of the Dinosaurs Templates

Tyrannosaurus

Collaborative Art & Writing Projects for Young Learners Scholastic Teaching Resources

Animals Around the World

Turn children's natural fascination with animals into an opportunity to teach geography. In this 3-D project kids create a papier-mâché earth and then populate it by sculpting their favorite animals!

Book Links

Crinkleroot's Guide to Knowing Animal Habitats
by Jim Arnosky (Aladdin, 2000)
Text filled with facts and pictures with labels help young readers get to know the natural habitats of some favorite creatures. A visit to the woodland challenges children to find 24 animals that live there.

The Family of Earth by Schim Schimmel
(Northword Press, 2001)
Detailed, realistic illustrations help readers appreciate the different habitats that animals call home, and the idea that they all share the same planet.

The Water Hole by Graeme Base (Abrams, 2001)
Die-cut pages in this whimsical counting book introduce young readers to more than 100 animals from around the world.

Will We Miss Them? Endangered Species
by Alexandra Wright (Charlesbridge, 1991)
An 11-year-old author introduces different endangered animals and explains why they are in jeopardy, in this Reading Rainbow selection.

Web Site

World Wildlife Fund
www.worldwildlife.org
The WildFinder feature on this site lets users search by species or place to find out who lives where. Detailed information is provided on endangered animals, including

Getting Started

1. Help your class learn about animals from different parts of the world. Share the books listed in Book Links, or visit the Web site, left. (Always supervise children's use of the Internet.) Discuss with children the ways in which the animals are adapted to the habitats in which they live. For example, rain forest frogs have long legs for jumping and suction cups on their toes for gripping slippery surfaces. Penguins have thick layers of fat, called blubber, that keep them warm in very cold environments. Giraffes have long necks, perfect for reaching leafy treetops to nibble on.

2. Compile a list of animals from around the world and the kinds of habitats in which they live. Discuss with your class the part of the world in which each animal lives. (Make sure children understand that animals often live in more than one area.) To set the stage for the art project, check that the list includes animals that live in very different areas, such as penguins (Antarctica and the Galápagos Islands off South America), pandas (China), sloths (rain forests in South America), giraffes and lions (different parts of Africa), elephants (different parts of Africa and Asia), kangaroos (Australia), and whales (various oceans).

Making the Globe

1. Cover a work area with newspaper. In a bowl, prepare the papier-mâché paste by mixing equal parts of flour and water until smooth. Then pour the paste into shallow containers. Set out more newspaper and a large round inflated balloon or beach ball, and a wide shallow container to serve as a base.

2. Divide the class into small groups. Let each group take a turn working at the papier-mâché work area. Demonstrate the papier-mâché process:

- Set the balloon or ball in the container to keep it steady.

- Rip newspaper into small strips, about 1 by 6 inches.

- Dip a paper strip into the paste, lay the strip on the balloon or ball, then smooth it out.

- Continue adding strips and paste, making sure they overlap. Build up two or three layers of strips.

- Allow the papier-mâché to dry thoroughly.

Materials ———————

- newspaper
- large plastic bowl
- large spoon
- flour
- water
- shallow containers (paper bowls or styrofoam trays)
- extra-large round balloon or beach ball
- empty, wide, shallow can or plastic container (for base)

Tips: *If the paste thickens as children work, add a little more water. For a faster cleanup, wipe up excess paste while still wet.*

Painting the Globe

1. Cover a work area with newspaper. Provide pencils, blue and green tempera paint in containers, paintbrushes, and a classroom globe.

2. Let each group have a turn working at the globe-painting area. Have children set the papier-mâché globe on its base. Then, using the classroom globe as a reference, children use pencils to draw the landforms, oceans, and seas on the papier-mâché globe. Erase and adjust pencil lines as necessary.

3. Instruct them to paint the landforms green and the seas blue. Allow the paint to dry thoroughly.

Materials ———————

- pencils
- erasers
- tempera paints (blue and green)
- paint containers (paper plates, bowls, or styrofoam trays)
- paintbrushes
- classroom globe

Materials ━━━━━━━

- 1½-inch balls of air-drying clay*
- toothpicks
- tempera paints (in assorted colors)
- paint containers (paper plates, bowls, or styrofoam trays)
- paintbrushes

━━━━━━━━━━━━

Tip: *Model Magic brand works well for this project because it is particularly lightweight when dry and can easily be glued to the globe.*

Animals

1. Have children work in small groups. Provide them with air-drying clay and toothpicks.

2. Invite children to select an animal to mold. Show them how to roll the clay under their palms and pinch the material with their fingers to form their animals. Children can use a toothpick to make eyes or add features such as fur.

3. When the clay is dry, invite children to paint their animals.

Materials ━━━━━━━

- construction paper strips (2½ by 3½ inches)
- pencils or markers
- coffee stirrers or drinking straws, cut in half
- scissors

━━━━━━━━━━━━

Writing Connection: Name and Habitat Flags

1. Provide each group with construction paper strips, pencils or markers, stirrers or straws., and scissors.

2. Invite children to write or dictate the name of their animal and its habitat on one side of their "flag." On the reverse side, have them write a couple of words that describe the animal's habitat.

3. Snip two slits in each flag and then slide a stirrer or straw (flattened slightly) in and out of the slits.

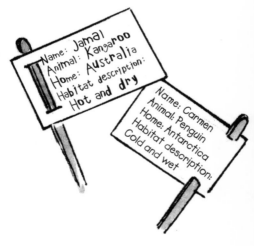

Materials ━━━━━━━

- glue

━━━━━━━━━━━━

To Assemble

1. Work with children individually to position the animals and descriptive flags in the appropriate locations. Use the point of a pencil (adult only) to poke small holes in the globe where each flag will go. Then have children glue their animal beside its corresponding flag.

2. Display your animals of the world and invite each child to talk about his or her animal and the habitat in which it lives.

Readable Railroad

From engines to cabooses, trains carry cars that are suited for different jobs. Some train cars carry passengers. Others carry cargo, such as coal. In this project, children use recycled materials such as boxes, tubes, and lids to construct a variety of train cars and then write about the special job of each.

Getting Started

1. Ask children if they have ever ridden on a train. What kind of train was it? Where did it take them? Children may be most familiar with commuter trains and subways. To introduce them to the many kinds of trains and the specific functions of different train cars, share some of the resources listed in Book Links, right.

2. After reading, ask children to name and describe some of the different kinds of train cars they read about. On chart paper, make a list of their responses. Then tell them they are going to build a train made up of the many different cars they learned about.

Tip: *This project can be done over three days (or three sessions), with children working in small groups. First, construct the train cars, then paint them, and finally assemble the cars to make one long train.*

Book Links

The Best Book of Trains by Richard Balkwill (Larousse Kingfisher Chambers, 1999)
This reference book gives a historical overview of trains and locomotion, from eighteenth-century railroads through steam engines to today's high-speed vehicles.

Hello, Freight Train! by Marjorie Blain Parker (Cartwheel, 2005)
Rhyming text and colorful illustrations bring a freight train to life—and inform young readers about the function of each car, from flatcars and boxcars to tank cars, refrigerator cars, and more.

The Little Train by Lois Lenski (Random House, 2000)
As Engineer Small runs his train from Tinytown to the city and back, readers learn details about a working train—its journey, cargo, and passengers.

Steam, Smoke, and Steel: Back in Time with Trains by Patrick O'Brien (Charlesbridge, 2000)
Seven generations of train engineers provide the story frame for exploring the history of locomotives from the 1830s to the present.

Trains by Anne Rockwell (Anne Rockwell's Transportation Series)
Colorful, appealing illustrations enhance simple text to tell about a variety of trains, including freight and passenger trains, subways, and monorails.

Materials

- cardboard boxes (cereal, tea, crackers, and so on)
- bathroom tissue and paper towel rolls
- lids (jars, juice cans, yogurt lids)
- bottle caps
- glue
- scissors
- coupler template, page 41

Making the Train Cars

1. Provide children with a variety of empty cardboard boxes and rolls, lids, caps, scissors, and glue.

2. Demonstrate how children can combine boxes, rolls, lids, and caps to create different kinds of cars. For example, a paper towel tube works well as a tank car, a long cracker box with the lid cut off can carry coal, and small pieces cut from bathroom tissue rolls can be used to make a smokestack on a steam engine. Bottle caps or jar lids make wheels.

3. Let children glue the pieces together.

 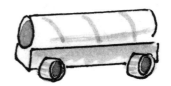 

4. Give children coupler templates to trace and cut out from construction paper. (These will be used to hook the train cars to each other.) Have children punch holes in the couplers as shown. Then have them glue the couplers to each end of the train cars, on the bottom. Let the glue dry.

Materials

- tempera paint (assorted colors)
- shallow paint containers (paper plates, bowls, or styrofoam trays)
- paintbrushes
- construction paper (assorted colors)
- markers

Painting the Train Cars

1. Provide children with tempera paint in containers, paintbrushes, construction paper, and markers.

2. Invite children to paint their train cars. Let the paint dry completely.

3. Children who have made engines, passenger cars, or cabooses can cut out paper windows and draw people on them to add later on.

Materials

- train car sentence frames, page 41
- scissors
- thin markers

Writing Connection: Train Car Sentence Frames

1. Copy and cut apart enough sentence frames for each train car.

2. Help children complete the sentence frame with an appropriate response—for example, *This car is carrying coal* or *This car is carrying passengers.*

To Assemble

1. Provide children with glue, brass fasteners, black licorice drops to represent lumps of coal, and cotton balls for steam engine smoke.

Materials

- glue
- brass fasteners
- black licorice drops (coal)
- cotton balls (steam engine smoke)

2. Have children glue windows with people drawn on them to passenger and engine cars, add licorice coal to open coal cars, and glue teased-apart cotton balls to the smokestack on the steam engine.

3. Show children how to link up the train cars by connecting the couplers using brass fasteners.

4. Let children glue their completed sentence frames to the sides of the train cars.

5. Clear an area of the floor to display the train. Then invite children to read aloud their Readable Railroad—Toot! Toot!

Train Car Sentence Frames

This car is carrying _____.

This car is carrying _____.

This car is carrying _____.

This car is carrying _____.

This car is carrying _____.

coupler template

What Grows on a Farm?

Turn your classroom into a farmers' market with fruits, vegetables, and flowers you create. Then have your young farmers work collaboratively to write catchy jingles for marketing their goods.

Book Links

Apple Farmer Annie by Monica Wellington
(Dutton, 2001)
Apple farmer Annie picks apples to make applesauce, apple muffins, apple cake, and apple cider. After selling everything at the market, she comes home to eat her own apple. This book features bright illustrations and recipes!

Farmers' Market by Paul Brett Johnson
(Orchard, 1997)
Get up before dawn with Laura and her family as they pack up their truck and head off to the farmers' market to sell their vegetables. A double-page spread opens to a lively poster-size picture that shows the sights Laura sees as she strolls through the market. Vivid illustrations bring the market to life.

Farmer's Market: Families Working Together by
Cheryl Walsh Bellville (Carolrhoda, 2001)
Colorful photographs help tell the story of a farmers' market, including two farming families—one Hmong and the other Polish-German—who grow the food.

Growing Vegetable Soup by Lois Ehlert
(Harcourt, 1990)
This vibrant book introduces the gardening cycle, from planting seeds and pulling weeds to picking vegetables and making soup, and includes an easy-to-make recipe.

Getting Started

1. Read about farmers' markets with your class by sharing some of the titles in Book Links, left. Then ask, "How are these markets different from grocery stores where people shop for food?" (*For example, farmers sell directly to customers freshly picked crops that they've grown; fruits and vegetables are usually not packaged in plastic or trays, which cuts down on trash; crops are often organic—grown without pesticides that might be harmful.*)

2. If possible, take a class field trip to a local farmers' market. Help children identify the fruits and vegetables they see. Encourage them to ask the farmers questions about how they grow their crops and what they choose to grow.

3. Divide the class into four groups. Assign each group a vegetable or fruit to create. One group will "grow" corn, another carrots, another peas, and another apples.

Corn

1. Provide children with corn and husk templates, pencils, yellow and green construction paper, scissors, cardboard scraps, glue, and popcorn.

2. Show children how to trace the corn template onto yellow construction paper, the husk template onto green construction paper, and then cut out the shapes. Have them repeat again and again for a bountiful corn harvest.

3. Let children use scraps of cardboard to spread glue on the yellow paper corn.

4. Show them how to overlap the edges of the corn with the green paper husks and press firmly to hold in place.

5. Have children sprinkle popcorn kernels onto the yellow corn section. Let the glue dry.

Materials ━━━━━━━
- **corn and husk templates, page 46**
- **pencils**
- **construction paper (yellow and green)**
- **scissors**
- **cardboard scraps**
- **glue**
- **unpopped popcorn kernels**

━━━━━━━━━━━

Carrots

1. Provide children with carrot templates, pencils, orange construction paper, scissors, green crepe paper, and tape.

2. Show children how to trace the carrot template onto the orange construction paper and then cut out the shape. Have them repeat to harvest more carrots.

3. To add the leafy tops, have them staple three pieces of the green crepe paper streamers together at one end. Use tape to secure to the wide end of the carrot shape, as shown.

4. Model how to overlap the long sides of the orange paper, curling it to create a narrow cone shape, and then use tape to secure.

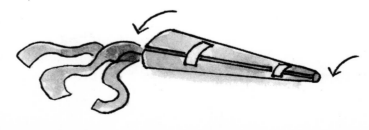

Materials ━━━━━━━
- **carrot template, page 47**
- **pencils**
- **orange construction paper**
- **scissors**
- **green crepe paper streamers, cut into 6-inch lengths**
- **stapler**
- **tape**

━━━━━━━━━━━

Materials ▬▬▬▬▬▬

- **pea pod template, page 47**
- **pencils**
- **9- by 12-inch green construction paper**
- **scissors**
- **4-inch squares of green tissue paper**
- **glue**
- **green pipe cleaners, cut in half**
- **hole punch**

▬▬▬▬▬▬▬▬▬▬

Peas

1. Provide children with pea pod templates, pencils, green construction paper, scissors, green tissue paper, glue, green pipe cleaners, and a hole punch.

2. Show children how to trace the pea pod template onto green construction paper and then cut out the shape. Have them repeat this process again and again to harvest more pea pods.

3. Demonstrate how to crumple green tissue paper squares to form round peas. Then glue three or four peas to one side of the pea pod. Let the glue dry.

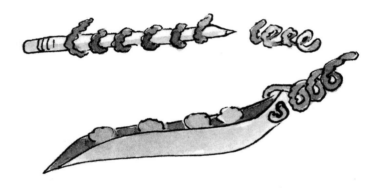

4. Show children how to curl a pipe cleaner half around a pencil to create a curly vine.

5. Model how to bring both sides of the pea pod together and punch a hole at one end through layers of paper. Poke one end of the pipe cleaner through the hole and fold over to secure in place.

Materials ▬▬▬▬▬▬

- **newspaper**
- **masking tape**
- **red tempera paint**
- **paint containers (paper plates, bowls, or styrofoam trays)**
- **paintbrushes**
- **apple leaf template, page 47**
- **pencils**
- **green construction paper**
- **scissors**
- **hole punch**
- **green pipe cleaners, cut in half**

▬▬▬▬▬▬▬▬▬▬

Apples

1. Provide children with newspaper, masking tape, red tempera paint in containers, paintbrushes, apple leaf templates, pencils, green construction paper, scissors, a hole punch, and green pipe cleaners.

2. Show children how to crumple newspaper to create a round apple shape and then secure the shape with masking tape. Repeat again and again to harvest more apples.

3. Have children paint the apples with red tempera. Allow the paint to dry thoroughly.

4. Show children how to trace the leaf template onto the green construction paper, cut out the shape, and then punch a hole for a stem.

5. Next, they bend the pipe cleaner in half, poke it through the leaf, and twist the ends together to form the stem. Finally, they poke the stem into the apple, at the top, near the center.

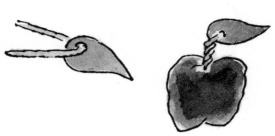

Writing Connection: Persuasive Writing

Materials ━━━━━━━
- **white paper**
- **pencils or markers**
- **paper plates, bowls, or baskets**
━━━━━━━━━━━━

1. Encourage children to recall jingles and slogans they have heard on television or radio commercials. What do jingles and slogans do? (*These advertisements help people become familiar with and buy particular products.*) Why are they effective? (*People hear them over and over and remember their catchy wording or tunes.*)

2. Let children work in groups to write a song, jingle, or slogan to sell their produce. Ask the farmers to describe their product. How can they convince someone to buy it? Have children write or dictate their ideas.

3. Host a farmers' market in your classroom. Bring in containers for displaying the produce. Invite other classes and family members to shop for vegetables and fruit. Let your farmers share their jingles and slogans to sell their harvest bounty!

Apples! Apples!
Come quick and buy!
They're tasty fresh,
in applesauce or pie.

Crisp and snappy,
Our crunchy peas—
They'll make you happy.
Buy some please!

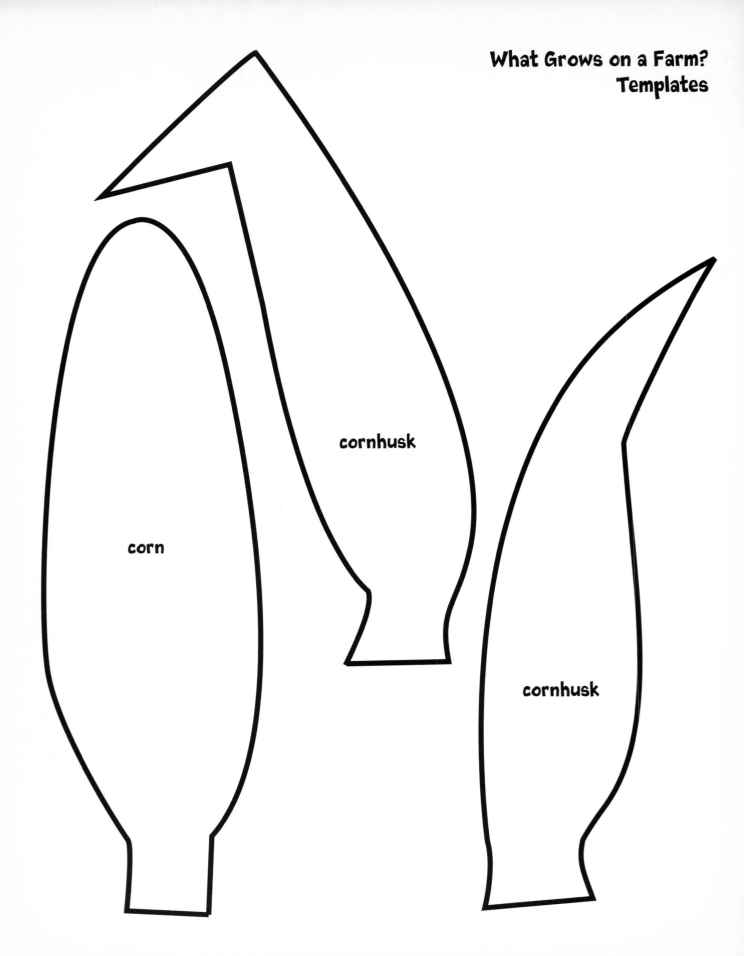

corn

cornhusk

cornhusk

Collaborative Art & Writing Projects for Young Learners Scholastic Teaching Resources

What Grows on a Farm? Templates

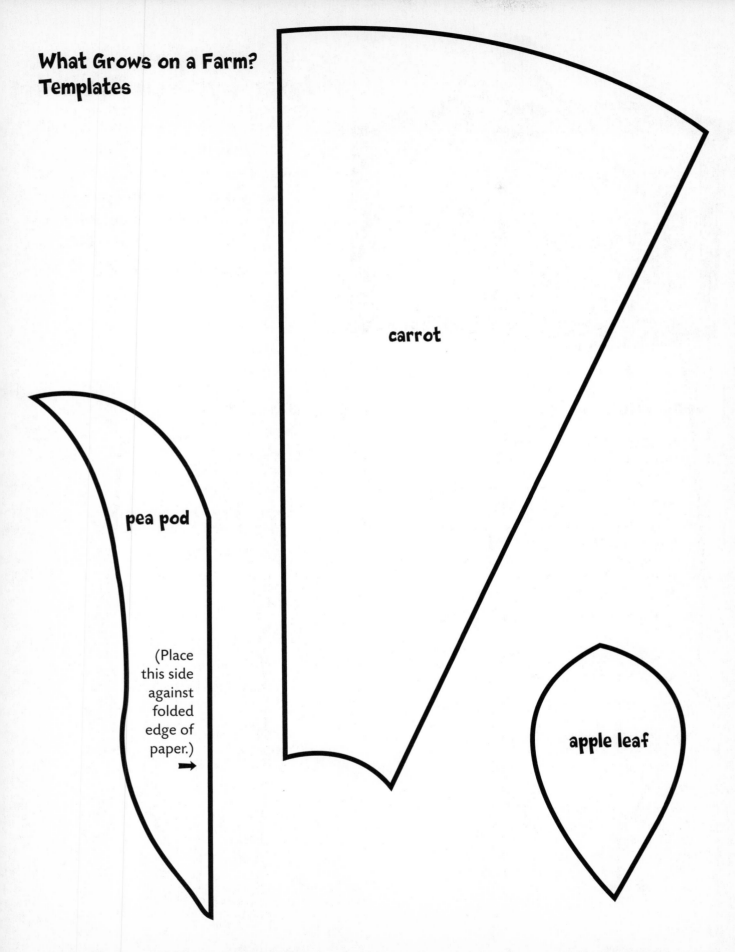

carrot

pea pod

(Place this side against folded edge of paper.) ➡

apple leaf

Water Cycle Go-Round

In this project, glue-resist chalk drawings give the illusion of water—perfect for illustrating the phases of the water cycle. Then children explore onomatopoeia by capturing the sounds of the water cycle in writing.

Book Links

Down Comes the Rain by Franklyn M. Branley (HarperTrophy, 1997)
Learn how clouds form, why rain and hail happen, and more. Key vocabulary is defined in context, and simple science activities invite hands-on exploration.

A Drop Around the World by Barbara Shaw McKinney (Dawn Publications, 1998)
Written in verse, this innovative book follows one raindrop around the world—from Maine to Mumbai—to explore the connection to life on earth.

The Drop Goes Plop: A First Look at the Water Cycle by Sam Godwin (Picture Window Books, 2004)
Join a mother and baby gull as they follow the journey of a drop of water. Fun facts and useful words provide additional information in this First Look: Science title.

A Drop of Water: A Book of Science and Wonder by Walter Wick (Scholastic 1997)
Spectacular photographs invite readers to observe water as ice, steam, rainbow, frost, and dew—and learn about related concepts including condensation and evaporation.

Water, Water Everywhere by Mark J. Rauzon and Cynthia Overbeck Bix (Sierra Club Books for Children, 1995)
Beginning with the glorious image on the cover, this book is filled with photographs that celebrate the wonder of water.

Getting Started

I. Find out what children know about the water cycle by asking questions, such as "What are clouds made of? Where does rain come from? What happens to puddles after it rains?" Then help children begin to explore this fascinating and remarkable process by sharing some of the stories and nonfiction books suggested in Book Links, left. Afterward, review with children the steps in the water cycle:

- The sun warms the water in oceans, rivers, and lakes.
- The water turns into water vapor—an invisible gas—and rises into the air.
- In the sky, the water vapor collects and forms a cloud.
- When a cloud becomes full of water vapor, the vapor turns into droplets and falls as rain or snow.
- The process then repeats itself, over and over.

2. Explain to children that they are going to use what they learned to illustrate each part of the water cycle.

Tip: *Divide the class into small groups and invite the children in each group to illustrate pages of one step in the water cycle.*

Background

1. About two inches from the top of each sheet of paper, draw a line lightly in pencil.

2. Cover work areas with newspaper. Assign each group a step in the water cycle to illustrate. Then provide the children in each group with paper and glue.

3. Invite children to illustrate this step in pencil in the area below the line. Encourage them to think about the way rain falls, water ripples, waves move, and so on.

4. Show children how to use glue to draw over the water areas in their illustration. Allow the glue to dry completely.

Materials ━ ━ ━ ━ ━ ━
- ruler
- pencil
- newspaper
- 7- by 9-inch sheets of white construction paper
- glue
━ ━ ━ ━ ━ ━ ━ ━ ━ ━

Water and Rain

1. Provide each group with colored chalk or pastels in a variety of blues and greens.

2. Show children how to color over the glue drawings with the chalk or pastels. Encourage heavy application of colors to make the glue resist stand out. Children can use their fingers to blend and spread the colors.

Materials ━ ━ ━ ━ ━ ━
- chalk or pastels (in assorted blues and greens)
━ ━ ━ ━ ━ ━ ━ ━ ━ ━

Materials ━━━━━━━

- white paper
- thin black markers

CRASHETY KABOOM!
Thunder cracks and roars.
Pitter-patter, plop!
Clouds pour down the rain.

Materials ━━━━━━━

- 1½- by 9-inch strips of white construction paper
- glue stick
- scissors

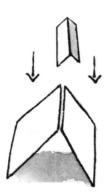

Writing Connection: Using Onomatopoeia

1. Ask children to think of words that describe the sounds of water: for example, *gurgle* might describe the sound of water flowing in a stream; *crash* might be ocean waves hitting the shore, while *ping, plop, ping* might be rain hitting a roof. Point out that these words sound like their meanings.

With children, brainstorm a list of other words to describe water that sound like what they mean, such as *drip, whoosh, slosh, pitter-patter, trickle, rush, plink, split-splat,* and *splish-splash.*

2. Ask children to think about words to describe the step in the water cycle their artwork illustrates. Have them write or dictate their descriptions on a sheet of white paper. Encourage them to use words that sound like water in its different forms.

To Assemble

1. To create hinges, fold 1½- by 9-inch strips of white paper in half the long way, as shown.

2. Help children organize the illustrations to show the complete water cycle.

3. Turn the glue-resist illustrations facedown and line them up side by side.

4. Using a glue stick, attach the hinges to the back of the prints, where the two prints meet.

5. Cut out individial student writings and glue one or more to each page, matching the writings with the water cycle artwork.

6. Stand up the hinged drawings and arrange them in a circle to emphasize the ongoing nature of the water cycle. Join the first page to the last page.

7. Have a class reading complete with sound effects!

Perky Penguins

Children use collage and printing to create the icy and watery world of penguins, providing the perfect background for writing about these unique and fascinating birds.

Getting Started

1. Begin the project by finding out what children know about penguins and what they would like to learn. Create a KWL (Know, Want to Know, Learned) chart to record children's responses. Then help children learn about penguins—the environment in which they live, their life cycles, social behavior, feeding habits, and more. See the resources in Book Links and the Web site, below. (Always supervise children's use of the Internet.)

2. After doing reading and research, refer to the KWL chart and ask children to share some of the facts they learned. Record their responses. Then tell children that this research will help them create a book in which they can share the wealth of information they learned.

Tip: *Do this project over three days or three sessions, with children working in small groups.*

Book Links

Antarctic Antics: A Book of Penguin Poems by Judy Sierra (Gulliver, 1998)
This book is an ideal read-aloud of 13 whimsical penguin poems, combined with factual information and comical illustrations.

The Emperor's Egg by Martin Jenkins (Candlewick, 2002)
This playful look at penguins invites readers to imagine what it would be like to be a male emperor penguin and spend two months with an egg on your feet.

Penguin Chick by Betty Tatham (HarperCollins, 2002)
Watch an emperor penguin grow from egg to adulthood, plus find facts about five species and learn to walk and toboggan like a penguin!

Penguins! by Gail Gibbons (Holiday House, 1999)
Meet 17 species of penguins, and learn where they live (pinpointed on a map of the southern hemisphere), what they eat, and more.

Penguins: Growing Up Wild by Sandra Markle (Atheneum, 2002)
This photo-essay describes the life of the Adelie penguin: mating, nest building, egg laying, incubation, and development into adulthood. A glossary explains important vocabulary.

Web Site

National Geographic.Com Kids
www.nationalgeographic.com/kids/creature_feature/0101/penguins.html
Find facts about penguins, watch a video, locate penguin homes on a map, send a penguin postcard, even tackle a penguin brainteaser at this fun-filled site.

Materials ————————

- newspaper
- foam rollers with plastic handles (available at craft or paint stores)
- 12-inch lengths of string
- tempera paint (blue and white)
- shallow paint containers (styrofoam trays)
- tissue paper in large sheets (in assorted blues)

————————

Water

1. Cover children's work areas with newspaper. Provide each group with foam rollers wrapped with string, containers of blue and white tempera paints, extra empty trays, and tissue paper in assorted blue colors.

2. Ask children to describe the environment in which many kinds of penguins live (*cold, icy, watery*). Then demonstrate how to paint with the rollers:

   - Roll a string-wrapped roller through a shallow tray of paint.
   - In an empty tray, roll off excess paint.
   - On a sheet of tissue paper, roll along the entire length of the paper in one direction only.

3. Ask children what the curving and repeating patterns of string resemble (*water*). Then invite them to cover the sheets of tissue paper with string-roll prints. (Avoid mixing colors by designating one roller for white paint and another roller for blue.) Allow the paint to dry.

Materials ————————

- newspaper
- 11-inch by 12-foot white bulletin board paper
- ruler
- pencil
- glue and water mixture (equal amounts of each)
- shallow containers (paper plates, bowls or styrofoam trays)
- paintbrushes
- 9- by 12-inch piece of white posterboard (for front cover)

————————

Background

1. Cover a work area on the floor with newspaper. Spread out the bulletin board paper. Measure eight inches in from each end and lightly pencil a vertical line. Then fold the paper back along this line at each end.

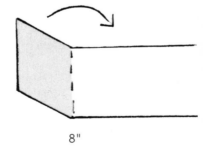

8"

2. Provide a container of the glue and water mixture, paintbrushes, and the string-printed tissue paper.

3. Have children tear the string-printed tissue into small pieces and paint the reverse side of each piece with glue.

4. Direct them to attach the torn tissue pieces along the entire lower half of the paper to represent water. Encourage children to alternate colors of blue, allow the pieces to overlap, and to leave some areas white (to represent ice).

5. Repeat this process on the posterboard for the front cover which will be attached later.

Penguins

1. Cover work area with newspaper. Provide children with the flat pieces of styrofoam, pencils or ballpoint pens, foam rollers, containers of black tempera paint, a nonabsorbent inking surface (such as a cookie sheet or waxed paper), white construction paper, and wooden spoons.

2. Invite children to illustrate a scene depicting penguin behavior on the flat styrofoam—for example, penguins swimming, diving, waddling, or catching food. To draw their picture, they should firmly press a pencil or ballpoint pen into the styrofoam.

3. Demonstrate relief printing:

- Dip a roller in black tempera paint and then coat a nonabsorbent inking surface with the paint, spreading it evenly.

- Roll the paint-filled roller across a sample styrofoam drawing, covering the surface with paint.

- Place a sheet of paper on the styrofoam drawing and rub the surface of the paper with a wooden spoon to make a print on the paper.

- Remove the paper carefully by one corner to reveal the finished print. Hang or store flat to dry.

4. Repeat steps 2–3 on the front cover.

Materials ━━━━━━

- **newspaper**
- **flat pieces of styrofoam (trays with curved sides removed)**
- **pencils or ballpoint pens**
- **foam rollers with plastic handles (available at craft or paint stores)**
- **black tempera paint**
- **shallow paint containers (styrofoam tray)**
- **nonabsorbent inking surface (cookie sheets or waxed paper)**
- **white construction paper**
- **wooden spoons**
- **front cover (See Materials, bottom of page 52.)**

━━━━━━━━

Materials ━━━━━━━

• white paper
• thin black markers

━━━━━━

Penguins huddle around their babies.

Penguins eat Fish.
Penguins eat Shrimp.
Penguins eat Krill.

Writing Connection:
Nonfiction Penguin Book

Ask each child to share a fact that he or she learned about penguins and then record or dictate this information on a sheet of white paper. To help children get started, prompt them with topics such as the following:

• physical characteristics, such as coloration and markings
• adaptations to harsh, icy habitats
• life cycles and nesting behavior
• feeding habits
• ways they move
• how they stay safe from predators
• ways of catching food

Materials ━━━━━━━

• ruler
• scissors
• glue
• 9- by 12-inch piece of white posterboard (for back cover)
• 4-foot piece of yarn or ribbon

To Assemble

1. Fanfold the long collaged paper to create 8½- by 11-inch pages. Unfold and spread flat again. The page creases will serve as guides when positioning additional elements.

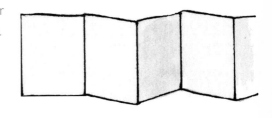

2. Cut out the penguin prints and glue them onto the collaged pages.

3. Cut out individual student writings and glue one or more to each collaged page, matching the writings with the penguin artwork.

4. Glue the previously prepared front cover and the back cover to the backs of the first and last pages. Allow the glued elements to dry.

5. Refold the accordion book. Add a title on the front cover. To keep the book closed, tie with yarn or ribbon.

6. Put the book in a reading center and encourage children to visit, reread, and share the book with classmates.

Ants at Work

Kids will love this print and collage project in which they create an ant world complete with underground paths, chambers, and a colony of fingerprint ants!

Getting Started

1. What do children know about ants? Have they ever seen ants? Where? What would they like to find out about these insects? Help children learn about the underground world of ants—their physical characteristics, social behavior, how they find food, build their homes, and more. See Book Links, right, for resources.

2. Invite children to share some of the facts they learned about ants. Write down their thoughts on chart paper. Then tell children that they are going to illustrate and write a book that will give a close-up look at these tiny but amazing insects.

Ant Facts

- Ants live in colonies.
- They dig tunnels and chambers under the ground
- The Queen ant lays eggs.
- Worker ants take care of the babies. They look for food, too.
- Ants are insects. They have six legs and three body parts.
- Ants don't see well. But they can see things move.
- Ants don't have ears, a tongue, or a nose. They use their antennae to hear, taste, smell, and touch.
- If you were as strong as the strongest ant, you could lift three horses!

Book Links

Ant Cities by Arthur Dorros (HarperCollins, 1982)
This Reading Rainbow selection explores the way ants work together to clean the nest, dig tunnels, gather food, and more.

Are You an Ant? by Judy Allen (Kingfisher, 2002)
See the world from an ant's point of view and learn about how they grow, what they eat, and how they protect themselves.

Inside an Ant Colony by Allan Fowler (Children's Press, 1998)
Watch ants digging tunnels and more with the fascinating photographs in this book from the Rookie Read-About Science series.

Thinking About Ants by Barbara Brenner (Mondo, 1996)
Text framed as questions engages young readers in discovering answers in this close-up look at ants. Different species of ants are identified in an appendix.

Tip: *Do this project over four days or sessions, with children working in small groups on different sections.*

Materials

- newspaper
- 11-inch by 12-foot white bulletin board paper
- ruler
- pencil
- sponges
- tempera paint (yellow, brown, black, orange, gold, and green)
- shallow paint containers (paper plates, bowls, or styrofoam trays)
- plastic forks
- 9- by 12-inch piece of white posterboard (for front cover)

Background

1. Cover a work area on the floor with newspaper. Spread out the bulletin board paper. Measure eight inches in from each end and lightly pencil a vertical line. Then fold the paper back along this line at each end.

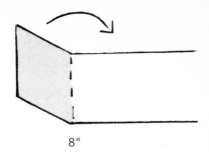

8"

2. Provide sponges and containers of yellow, brown, black, orange, and gold tempera for printing the earth and plastic forks and containers of green paint for printing the grass.

3. Demonstrate how to dip a sponge in paint and use it to print on the paper. Then invite children to make earthlike prints along the entire lower half of the paper. Remind them to keep colors pure by using a separate sponge for each color.

4. To print blades of grass, show children how to dip a fork in green paint and then press it to the paper above the earth.

5. Repeat steps 3–4 on the posterboard for the front cover which will be attached later.

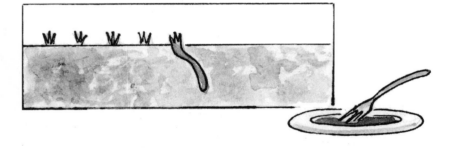

Materials

- brown paper bags
- glue
- paintbrushes
- front cover (See Materials, above)

Ant Tunnels

1. Provide children with brown paper bags, glue, and paintbrushes.

2. Invite them to tear the brown paper bags into different shapes to simulate underground paths and chambers.

3. Have children glue the paper bag paths and chambers on top of the printed earth area, all along the length of the paper. Let the glue dry.

4. Repeat steps 2–3 on the front cover.

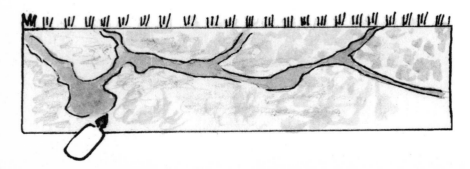

Ants

1. Provide children with containers of black and white paint, thin black markers, green and brown construction paper, scissors, and glue.

Materials ━ ━ ━ ━
- **tempera paint (black and white)**
- **shallow paint containers (paper plates, bowls, or styrofoam trays)**
- **thin black markers**
- **construction paper (green and brown)**
- **scissors**
- **glue**
- **front cover (See Materials, top of page 56.)**

━ ━ ━ ━ ━ ━ ━ ━

2. Ask, "How many body parts does an ant have?" (*three—the head, thorax, and abdomen*) Then show children how to create ant bodies by dipping the tip of their little finger in black paint and then printing on the collaged paper. They should dip and print three times for each complete ant body. Encourage children to print ants in the grass, underground paths, and chambers.

3. Ask, "How many legs does an ant have? How about antennae?" (*An ant has six legs and two antennae.*) Invite children to add legs and antennae, using thin black markers.

4. Ask, "What happens in ant chambers?" (*Ants lay their eggs.*) Children can dip their fingertips in white paint and then print to create eggs.

5. Ask, "What things might ants carry?" (*leaves, twigs, food*) Have children create these items using scissors and green and brown construction paper, and then glue them to the collage. Let the glue dry.

6. Repeat steps 2–5 on the front cover.

Materials ━━━━━━━

- white paper
- thin black markers

Writing Connection: All About Ants

1. Ask children to study the ant world they created—the tunnels, chambers, and the ants themselves. What do the details tell about ants and how they live?

2. Invite children to write or dictate captions that describe the scenes they illustrated. Encourage them to use vocabulary words they learned, such as *insect, tunnel,* and *chambers.*

> Ants live in chambers. Ants lay eggs.

> Ants carry twigs. Ants carry leaves.

> Some ants guard the nest.

Materials ━━━━━━━

- ruler
- glue
- scissors
- 9- by 12-inch piece of white posterboard (for back cover)
- 4-foot piece of yarn or ribbon

To Assemble

1. Fanfold the collaged paper to create 8½- by 11-inch pages. Unfold and spread flat again. The page creases will serve as guides when positioning additional elements.

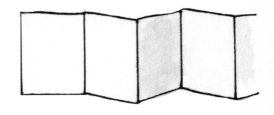

2. Tear around individual student writings and glue one or more to each page.

3. Glue the previously decorated front cover and the back cover to the backs of the first and last pages. Allow the glued elements to dry.

4. Refold the accordion book. Add a title on the front cover. To keep the book closed, tie with yarn or ribbon.

5. Put the book in a reading center and encourage children to visit, reread, and share the book with classmates.

Busy Bees

For this colorful and informative accordion book, children combine collage and printmaking to create a beautiful garden of torn paper flowers, dancing bees, and honeycombed hives.

Getting Started

1. Begin by asking children if they know where bees live. Then explain that some insects, such as wasps, ants, and bees, build their own homes. Bees, for example, build hives. Show children one of the hexagon templates (see page 62), and, together, count the sides. Explain that bees build hives that are made of thousands of six-sided shapes called cells. Together these cells form a honeycomb. Each cell is like a room in a home.

2. Help children learn about bee behavior, including how bees pick up pollen and nectar from flowers, produce honey in their hives, and dance in different patterns to communicate, as well as other characteristics of bees. Share some of the resources suggested in Book Links and the Web site, below. (Always supervise children's use of the Internet.)

Book Links

Beekeepers by Linda Oatman High (Boyds Mills Press, 1998) Watch beekeepers at work, as a girl and her grandfather put on protective gear and head to their hives to harvest honey.

Bumblebee at Apple Tree Lane by Laura Gates Galvin (Soundprint, 2000) Learn about life cycles as a bumblebee awakens from winter hibernation and spends spring and summer preparing the nest, laying eggs, and providing food for the larvae before returning to hibernation in the fall. This book comes with an audiocassette.

Honeybees by Deborah Heiligman (National Geographic, 2002) Part of the Jump into Science series, this book is packed with details about the life of bees—from how they develop to the many jobs they do.

The Honey Makers by Gail Gibbons (HarperCollins, 1997) Discover how bees make honey, explore their life cycle, and learn about the jobs worker bees do. Diagrams, captions, labels, and a fact page expand on the information presented.

The Magic School Bus Inside a Beehive by Joanna Cole (Scholastic, 1996) Board the bus with Ms. Frizzle and her students for a field trip inside a beehive. Take a tour of the hive, and learn how bees communicate, build hives, make honey, and more.

Web Site

Nature: Alien Empire–Enter the Hive www.pbs.org/wnet/nature/alienempire/multimedia/hive.html Take a virtual tour of a beehive, and learn about a bee's life, pollination, and honey.

Tip: This project can be done over three days (or three sessions). Begin with the garden background. Then make the flowers, bees, and hives. Finally assemble the parts to make an accordion book.

Materials —————

- newspaper
- 11-inch by 12-foot sheet of white bulletin board paper
- ruler
- pencils
- construction paper (assorted colors)
- hexagon templates, page 62
- scissors
- glue
- 9- by 12-inch piece of white posterboard (for front cover)

—————————————

Garden Background

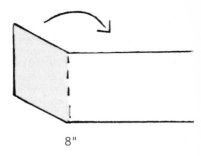

8"

1. Cover a work area on the floor with newspaper. Spread out the bulletin board paper. Measure 8 inches in from each end and lightly pencil a vertical line. Then fold the paper back along this line at each end.

2. Provide children with construction paper in assorted colors, hexagon templates, pencils, scissors, and glue.

3. Show children how to tear different colors of paper to form flowers and leaves for a garden for the bees.

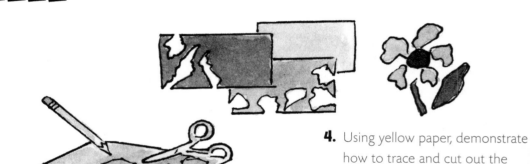

4. Using yellow paper, demonstrate how to trace and cut out the hexagon templates to create honeycomb shapes for the bees.

5. Direct children to work along the bottom half of the paper, filling the length of the paper with the collage paper flowers and cut honeycombs.

6. When children are satisfied with their arrangement, have them glue the elements to the background. Allow to dry.

7. Repeat steps 3–6 on the posterboard for the front cover which will be attached later.

Bees

1. Spread out the collage paper garden. Provide children with the halved potatoes, forks, plastic-coated wire bent into oval loops with handles (as shown), containers of yellow and black paint, black markers, and light blue pencils.

2. Demonstrate how to create bees: Dip the cut side of a potato half into yellow paint, and then stamp it onto the garden background.

3. Add stripes by dipping a fork into black paint and then using it to make a print across the yellow body of the bee.

4. To add wings, dip the plastic-coated wire loop into black paint and then make two prints close to the bee's body. Use a black marker to add a stinger.

5. Encourage children to add details to show what they know about the behavior of bees—for example, sipping nectar, picking up pollen, and making honey in their hive. Have children use light blue pencils to depict the dancing patterns that bees use to communicate.

6. Repeat steps 2–5 on the front cover.

Writing Connection: Busy Bee Book

1. Ask children to look carefully at the illustrations they created and to describe the scenes they see.

2. Invite children to write or dictate facts they learned about bees to accompany their illustrations. They might describe the process in which bees gather nectar from flowers to make honey back in their hives, the dances bees use to communicate with each other, their physical characteristics, and so on. Encourage children to use vocabulary words they learned, such as *hexagon*, *honeycomb*, *hive*, *pollen*, and *nectar*.

Materials

- small, red new potatoes, cut in half
- tempera paint (yellow and black)
- shallow paint containers (paper plates, bowls or styrofoam trays)
- forks
- plastic-coated wire in 9-inch lengths
- thin black markers
- light blue colored pencils
- front cover (See Materials, page 60.)

Materials

- white paper
- thin black markers

Worker bees can only sting once.

Bees dance to show other bees where the flowers are.

Materials

- ruler
- glue
- scissors
- **9- by 12-inch piece of white posterboard (for back cover)**
- **4-foot piece of yarn or ribbon**

To Assemble

1. Using a ruler as a straightedge, fanfold the collaged paper to create 8½- by 11-inch pages. Then unfold the paper and spread out flat again. (The page creases will serve as guides when positioning additional elements.

2. Tear around individual students' writings to add to the collage book. Glue one or more to each page. Allow the glue to dry completely, and then refold the accordion book.

3. Glue the previously decorated front cover and the back cover to the backs of the first and last pages. Allow the glued elements to dry.

4. Refold the accordion book. Add a title on the front cover. To keep the book closed, tie with yarn or ribbon.

5. Put the book in a reading center and encourage children to visit, reread, and share the book with classmates.

Hexagon Templates

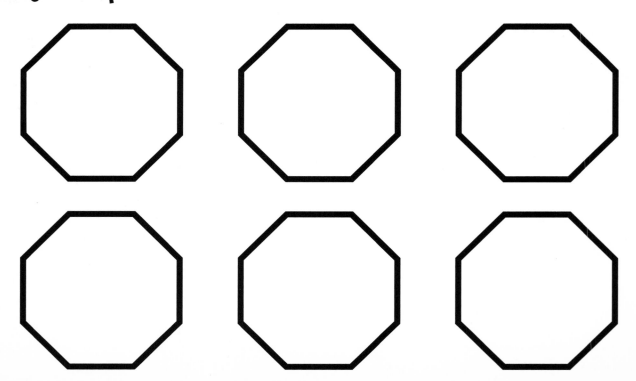

Butterfly Frieze

Invite children to explore the many sizes, shapes, and colors of butterflies with this simple-to-make print frieze. This project is also a great way to introduce symmetry and inspire poetry in your classroom.

Getting Started

1. Share books with children to introduce them to the many varieties of butterflies as well as their life cycle and migration habits. See Book Links and the Web site, below. (Always supervise children's use of the Internet.)

2. Show children pictures of different kinds of butterflies. Ask them to study the wings. What do they notice about them? (*The wings are symmetrical—each side matches the other side exactly.*) Then tell children that they will be making their own beautiful and symmetrical butterflies.

Book Links

Are You a Butterfly?
(Larousse Kingfisher Chambers, 2000)
Part of the Backyard Books series, this charming book invites young readers into a butterfly's world as it explains the stages of the butterfly's life cycle. Fact pages at the end of the book encourage further learning.

Butterfly House by Eve Bunting (Scholastic, 1999)
A young girl rescues a caterpillar, and, together with her grandfather, turns a box into a butterfly house bursting with painted flowers. Readers can watch alongside the girl as the metamorphosis takes place and a Painted Lady butterfly emerges and is set free.

Waiting for Wings by Lois Ehlert (Harcourt, 2001)
Written in rhyme and illustrated with vibrant cut-paper pictures, this dazzling book brings a butterfly's life cycle to life.

Wings of Change by Franklin Hill (Illumination Arts, 2001)
Explore concepts of change along with a contented caterpillar that doesn't want to grow into a butterfly.

Young Naturalist Pop-Up Handbook: Butterflies
by Robert Sabuda and Matthew Reinhart (Hyperion, 2001)
With the pull of a tab, caterpillars transform into butterflies that flutter about the pages of this informative and eye-catching pop-up book. A model butterfly specimen is a bonus for young collectors.

Web Site

Journey North: A Global Study of Wildlife Migration and Seasonal Change
www.learner.org/jnorth/
Join Journey North in tracking the migration patterns and routes of monarch butterflies. This site includes extensive teaching materials and detailed connections to science and math standards.

Materials

- newspaper
- 9- by 18-inch sheets of white paper
- tempera paints in assorted colors
- shallow paint containers (paper plates, bowls, or styrofoam trays)
- paintbrushes

Butterflies

1. Divide the class into small groups. Cover work surfaces with newspaper. Provide each group with white paper, containers of paint, and paintbrushes.

2. Model how to fold a sheet of white paper in half the short way and then reopen it.

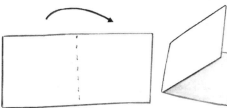

3. On one half of the paper, demonstrate how to paint butterfly wings using different colors of tempera. (Use a different brush for each color.)

4. Tell students to refold the paper, press it down with their hands, and then reopen it. What do they see? A complete butterfly! What else do students notice? *(Each side of their butterfly looks just like the other—the wings are symmetrical.)*

Writing Connection: Butterfly Poems

1. Choose a poetry exercise from the list below. On scrap paper, guide students to:

   - name their new species and write a descriptive word about it that begins with the same letter or shares a similar sound.
   - write a rhyming couplet about their butterfly.
   - create a free-verse poem about butterflies.
   - write a haiku about butterflies.

2. When children are satisfied with their poems, have them copy them onto their butterfly paintings.

> Purple, yellow, red, or pink,
> Nectar is your favorite drink!

Materials

- 1½- by 9-inch white paper strips
- glue sticks

To Assemble

1. To create hinges, fold 1½- by 9-inch strips of white paper in half the long way, as shown.

2. Turn the butterfly prints facedown and line them up side by side.

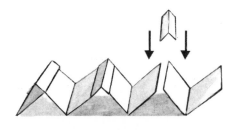

3. Using a glue stick, attach the hinges to the back side of the prints, where the two prints meet.

4. Display your butterfly frieze, and have a class poetry reading!